THE BOOK OF
THE WOOD PIGEON

By the same author

SPORT

Town Gun
Town Gun 2
Duck Shooting
The Gunpunt Adventure
The Angler's Encyclopædia
The ABC of Fishing (editor)
The ABC of Shooting (editor)
The Bedside Wildfowler (editor)

WILDLIFE AND TRAVEL

The Enormous Zoo
The Great Rift Valley
The World of Survival
Wildfight
Kingdom of the Deep
Kingdoms of the East

BIOGRAPHY AND AUTOBIOGRAPHY

Kenzie, the Wild Goose Man
Landscape with Solitary Figure

HUMOUR

Rod, Pole or Perch
Dudley, the Worst Dog in the World

FICTION

Death at Flight
Death at the Strike
Death in Covert
The Animal Catchers
Hazanda
The Coast of Loneliness
The Fighters
Gorilla
In the Rut

THE BOOK
OF THE
WOOD PIGEON
COLIN WILLOCK

with illustrations by

WILLIAM GARFIT

White Lion Books
CAMBRIDGE

White Lion Books
an imprint of
Colt Books Ltd
9 Clarendon Road
Cambridge, CB2 2BH
tel: 01223 329059   fax: 01223 65866

First published by White Lion Books 1995

ISBN 1 874762 16 3

British Library Cataloguing-in-Publication Data
A catalogue record for this book is available
from the British Library

Design by Clare Byatt

Printed in Great Britain by Biddles Ltd, Guildford.

CONTENTS

LIST OF ILLUSTRATIONS
by William Garfit

CHARTS
based on originals
by kind permission of MAFF

For Archie and Prue Coats

ACKNOWLEDGEMENTS

I THOUGHT I knew a lot about the wood pigeon until I came to write this book. I quickly discovered there was a lot I didn't know. So, first, my thanks to the scientific staff of the Game Conservancy Trust and the British Association for Shooting and Conservation. Both organisations are deeply involved in the wood pigeon research programme and yet they found time to talk at length and give me the benefit of their knowledge. So my thanks to Dr Dick Potts, Director of the Game Conservancy and Nicholas Aebisher, the Trust's Head of Biometrics. My special thanks to Dr Mike Swan of the Game Conservancy who read this manuscript, brought me up to date on aspects of modern agriculture, made many suggestions and corrections including the right use of the word 'decimate'. Equally, to John Swift, Director of BASC, who let me use his office and library, and to Dr John Harradine, Research Director of BASC who went to great trouble to meet me and talk about his research programme, even though his car had just broken down!

Dr Ian Inglis, of the Central Science Laboratory, who continues Dr Ron Murton's work at the wood pigeon study area at Carlton in Cambridgeshire, gave me a slant on many aspects of research into wood pigeon population dynamics. He also gave me permission to use some of the diagrams produced at the sweat of his and his field-workers' brows.

The mention of field-workers brings me to Tony Isaacson, senior scientific officer, now formally retired but still making winter population counts at Carlton. Tony and Peter Haynes, telemetry expert, spent a very hot day walking the woods and fields of Carlton. From Tony I learned much of the studies carried out there by Ron Murton and himself.

I am extremely grateful to John Ransford for letting me use his account of how he beat Archie Coats' pigeon record, and to the editor of *Shooting Times* for permission to reproduce John's story. Archie's account of his own big day is taken—by kind permission of Prue Coats and his publisher André Deutsch—from his book *Pigeon Shooting* now in its ninth edition. I thought that I knew a lot about Archie Coats, for whom this book is, I hope, in part a celebration. I discovered, however, that I knew less than three quarters of the whole Archie Coats story. Prue Coats happily and unstintingly told me the missing quarter. She also gave me permission to include some of her wonderful pigeon recipes. I thank Will Garfit, member of BASC's Wood Pigeon Working Party and ace pigeon shooter himself, not only for the illustrations he has done for this book but also for the enthusiasm he has typically shown for the project from the word 'go'.

Another member of that working party, John Batley, who makes his living entirely from shooting wood pigeons or teaching others to shoot them, was kindness itself, especially in view of the fact he was writing a pigeon shooting book himself at the time. John gave me much information relating to *les colombières*, the traditional hunters of wood pigeons migrating through the Pyrenees.

Finally, a debt of gratitude to Hungry Monk Publications, an off-shoot of that splendid restaurant at Jevington near Eastbourne, The Hungry Monk. I have long been an admirer of their cuisine. Now, thanks to *The Deeper Secrets of the Hungry Monk* I am able to reproduce two of their pigeon recipes.

INTRODUCTION

PRACTICALLY every other quarry species of British bird has had a book or even books devoted to its natural history, its problems, its sporting qualities and its pursuit. Since the days of *The Badminton Library* and the classic *Fur, Feather and Fin* series, both published a century ago, the great game birds, the pheasant, partridge and grouse, have all been enshrined in single volumes written by sportsman naturalists. Wildfowl, too, the ducks and geese have been given a similar accolade. The one exception to this form of literary recognition and celebration is a wild native bird that is more numerous in these islands than the rest of the quarry species put together. It is *Columba palumbus*, the wood pigeon.

True, the bird has been the subject of one classic scientific monograph by the late Dr R.K. Murton (*The Wood Pigeon*, Collins *New Naturalist* series). This stands alone as a unique, if now slightly outdated, record of research. And, even if I were capable of writing such a book, it is not what I have in mind at all.

Current figures suggest that at least a quarter of a million, and possibly as many as 300,000 guns regularly shoot wood pigeons. A few do so professionally. A small proportion—specialist sportsmen you might almost call them—do so with something approaching obsession. This writer is among them.

Unlike the game shooter, who is often more interested in his sport than his quarry, the pigeon shooter, amateur or professional, is invariably fascinated by his prey, its habits, its survival qualities, and how best he can adapt his own tactics and skills to outwit it. He knows that he has little chance of being consistently successful unless, in the words of the greatest professional wood pigeon shooter of them all, the late Archie Coats, he can 'think like a pigeon'. Success in the field depends largely on understanding the bird, its natural history, its feeding and flocking patterns. All this leads the pigeon shooter into seeking a wider knowledge of his quarry. I hope that this book will satisfy some of those needs as well as broadening the reader's interest in this most fascinating of wild birds.

There will, inevitably, be a section about shooting wood pigeons. But this is not a 'how-to-do-it' book. Others, notably Archie Coats (*Pigeon Shooting*, André Deutsch), John Humphreys (*Shooting Pigeons*, David and Charles) and John Batley (*The Pigeon Shooter*, Swan Hill Press), have already done that about as well as it can be done. So don't expect this book to teach you how to set out your decoys in a crosswind or put a 'lofter' thirty feet up in an ash tree. I will, however, tell in a narrative way the story of some different shoots, some big, some small, to illustrate the bird's natural wariness and on some occasions its amazing gullibility. The wood pigeon never fails to surprise even those who think they know every last thing about it. But then who does?

As I write, in 1994, it seems that there has never been a better moment at which to dedicate a book to this great bird. Two years ago the European Parliament in Brussels proposed to impose a close season for the wood pigeon that would last for about two thirds of the year. This would be binding on Britain as well as on its European partners. The suggestion was that the ban on shooting would start in March and end in November, thus covering all the main months in which the wood pigeon can, and often does, breed.

The quality of the eco-thinking behind the ban can be judged by the fact that the EU also proposed to award a fence season to the corvids so that the crow, the magpie and the jay could produce their destructive and already too-successfully proliferating young without human interference or any form of control. Shooters and naturalists were quick to point out that this seemed a strange, not to say inconsistent conservation strategy for a Community whose southern members, especially, shoot, net and lime, apparently without let or hindrance, millions of migrant songbirds for the table each spring and autumn.

The 300,000 wood pigeon shooters of Great Britain not surprisingly became extremely hot under the collars of their Barbour jackets and camouflaged smocks. So did British farmers, especially those who grow cereals, pulses and oilseed rape. The wood pigeon dearly loves all these valuable crops. In fact, the bird is adept at selecting for itself, often in flocks of several hundred strong, all that is best, most costly to grow and commercially valuable in the British countryside. For, among its other distinctions, the wood pigeon is this country's chief agricultural pest. It comes close to rivalling the rabbit when the latter is not suffering from a particularly virulent and widespread epedemic of myxomatosis.

Fortunately, the interests of both shooters and farmers were well represented in Brussels, though at one time it did look like touch and go. Those who fear for the eventual boiling down of Britain's sovereignty in the general European stockpot may take some heart, though perhaps only temporarily, from what happened in the case of the wood pigeon (also crow, magpie and jay). Representations from the Ministry of Agriculture, Fisheries and Food (MAFF), National Farmers Union (NFU), the British Association for Shooting and Conservation (BASC), the Game Conservancy Trust and others succeeded in forestalling the ban, though no one should be lulled into the belief that it has gone away for ever.

On 27 October, 1992, Lord Strathclyde read a Government Statement to the effect that the 'pest species' concerned would be put under an annual open general licence. In effect, this meant that wood pigeon and corvid control would continue in Britain exactly as if the European Community had never come up with their proposal for a close season. Moreover, no individual pigeon shooter need apply for a licence, or justify or account for the number of birds he shoots.

It was announced that these general licences, covering broad geographical areas, would be considered for renewal each year following advice from the government's statutory scientific advisors, the Joint Nature Conservation Committee

(JNCC). However, through these bodies Britain would be required to monitor the situation annually. Should there be any sign of a drastic decline in wood pigeon (or corvid) numbers, then the ban could well come into force.

When Chris Patten, then Environment Minister, announced that the wood pigeon would be shootable all the year round as before, many shooters cheered, believing that Britain had at last told the EU where to get off and was pre-pared to break an EU law to do so. This, satisfying as it might have been for some Euro-sceptic sportsmen and farmers, was just NOT the case. The proposed ban was an EU *Directive* which does not have the force of an EU Law. Had it become law, then Britain would have had no choice but to obey.

So, now we come to the crunch point and the reason why I feel this book is particularly timely. I said earlier in this introduction that the wood pigeon was one of the most scientifically studied birds in Britain. Most of that study has been carried out on a 2,600 acre MAFF study area at Carlton on the Cambridge–Suffolk border. The work begun by Dr Ron Murton in the 1950s and carried on to this day by his successors and, at this moment by Dr Ian Inglis and Tony Isaacson, was designed largely to learn the bird's effect on agriculture and, beyond that, possibly even to find an economic means of controlling it. The Carlton study has told us more about the wood pigeon than we know about most British birds but it still hasn't answered such key questions as: What is the total population of wood pigeon in Britain? Is the population increasing or declining? What affect, if any, does shooting have on protecting the farmer's crops? Does shooting keep numbers in check or even, though it seems extremely unlikely, cause the pigeon population to decline?

Now, obviously, if Britain is going to be pressurised in future years by the EU to take the wood pigeon off the shooting list for up to nine months in the year, answers to these questions have to be found. Those answers are, anyway, part of the monitoring process that we are required to carry out. It has to be said that there can be no doubt that if the wood pigeon population was found to be falling to a dangerously low level, through shooting or from natural causes, or from both, then everyone concerned, including the shooting community, would have to support appropriate protection for the bird. It is an unlikely eventuality. To try to provide the answers to the above questions—and no doubt many more besides—the British Association for Shooting and Conservation formed in 1993 a Wood Pigeon Working Party to counter 'what it perceived as a political threat to wood pigeon shooting as a sport and as a means of crop protection'.

In October 1993, The Working Party set up a Wood Pigeon Shooting Survey using some of BASC's 200,000 pigeon members to make returns of numbers shot, methods used, crops protected, etc. The objectives of the Survey (which is likely to continue for at least five years) include monitoring the pigeon population through numbers shot, quantifying the importance of the sport and demonstrating its relevance to crop protection.

BASC is not alone in this research programme. In parallel with its survey, the MAFF is carrying out its own analysis of ringing recoveries to determine how far changes in annual survival rates relate to changes in agriculture in Britain.

The Game Conservancy Trust is the third body integrated in this research plan. The Conservancy is interested in the pan-European view of the impact of shooting not only on the wood pigeon but on the other European members of the pigeon family, the stock dove, collared dove, and turtle dove.

The political situation in which the wood pigeon, the scientist, the farmer and the shooter now find themselves is reason enough to produce this book at this moment. But in truth, I have been longing to write such a book for a long time, and for purely personal reasons. Ever since I shot my first wood pigeon—with a ten-bore muzzle-loader!—in a clearing in a Sussex oak-wood in high summer some forty years ago, I have been one of the wood pigeon's greatest admirers.

Non-shooting people may find this hard to understand. What hypocrisy, they may say, for a man to claim to be in love with a bird when his freezers often contain a hundred or more of its ovenready corpses.

Ah, me! The ambivalence of the hunter. He can never explain the duality of his relationship with the creature he hunts. Admiration, respect are certainly part of it. So too is a healthy appreciation of a gourmet dish!

That first pigeon came at full throttle over the top of a bushy-topped oak in fresh June leaf. I had observed the flight-line, seen other pigeons use it, coming from I-knew-not-where and going I-knew-not-whither. In those days, it is obvious, that I knew very little about the daily habits of pigeons. I had tried unsuccessfully to shoot other pigeons with my newly acquired hundred-year-old gun, bought for a fiver. It was all I could afford in those days. The beautiful old gun was not at fault. It shot as sweetly then as when its maker put the finishing touches to its engraving.

I pulled the trigger. There was the gentle thud of a black powder discharge. The white smoke ballooned in the clearing. Amazingly, the pigeon folded its wings on the down-stroke, high above the treetops, and plummeted softly on to the grass almost at my feet.

Years ago, Peter Scott, analysing what, in his early days, fascinated him about shooting, said part of it was the act of possession, to be able to hold in the hand the creature that only seconds before was unobtainable. I know what he meant, even though I have not taken the path of conversion that he later trod, nor have I felt the need to.

With that first pigeon, I had taken possession of the previously unobtainable. I held the bird in my hand, wondering at the blush-pink of its breast, the creamy-white of its collar and wing markings, and the immaculate, morning-coat grey of its body plumage.

And I thought, then, what a splendid bird, an opinion I have held ever since and never expect to alter.

What They Said About
The Wood Pigeon

That naughty bird, *Columba palumbus*, the ring necked dove or wood pigeon, is indeed a bad boy and does a vast amount of harm to all members of the farming fraternity. He will also eat the greenstuff in your back garden as a sideline. Nevertheless, I am very fond of him, though I make my living out of his destruction .... *Archie Coats (Pigeon Shooting, 1963)*.

As some sort of recompense for the great damage it does to the crops, it must be remembered that the flesh of this bird is very palatable, and enormous numbers find their way into the markets .... *H. Seebohm (1884)*.

One of my neighbours shot a ring dove on an evening as it was returning from feed and going to roost. When his wife had picked and drawn it, she found its craw stuffed with the most nice and tender tops of turnips. These she washed and boiled, and so sat down to a choice plate of greens, culled and provided in this extraordinary manner. Hence we may see that granivorous birds, when grain fails, can subsist on the leaves of vegetables .... *Gilbert White (1720–1793)*.

A peculiarity common to the tame pigeon, the ring dove and the turtle dove is that they do not lean the head back when they are in the act of drinking, but only when they have fully quenched their thirst .... *Aristotle (from his Zoological Works, translated by D'Arcy W. Thompson, 1910)*.

The wood pigeon is a beautiful bird and were it not for its abundance and depredatory habits would almost certainly

I

receive the exaltation at present reserved for rare species ....
R.K. Murton (1965).

Wood pigeons are absolute gluttons. Just one bird devours:
enough strawberries in an hour to fill a large punnet; enough
Brussels in an afternoon to lunch a family of four; enough
barley in a day to brew a pint of beer; enough wheat in a week
to bake a large loaf; enough clover in a month to produce a
gallon of milk. In the south of England alone, wood pigeons
eat over 550 tons of food every day. So, when you down 'em
you're doing everybody a service that can be profitable as well
as fun .... *Eley cartridge pamphlet (Shooting Wood Pigeons, 1970).*

The wood pigeon emerges as a bird, indeed often a serious
pest, which must be lived with and understood; a bird with
an ineradicable (though changeable) niche in the process of
our European life .... *Editors, Collins New Naturalist (1965).*

Immigration takes place in the late autumn and winter,
when at times enormous flocks come into this area. They
have been seen to descend through the mist and settle among
the guelder rose berries like fog lamps on the marshes ....
E.A. Ellis (The Broads, 1965).

The wood pigeon can only be regarded as vermin. It is good
eating and it stands high in the estimation of shooting men
because it is extremely wary, flies high and flies fast .... But
the wood pigeon is not game in law; it is vermin in fact. It is
present in enormous numbers, it has an enormous appetite, it
will eat almost any plant apparently for the sake of eating.
It should have no close season. It should be destroyed, at
least until its numbers are within reasonable limits .... *Brian
Vesey-Fitzgerald (British Game, 1946).*

There is no kind of bird which tries more severely the nerve
and skill of those who delight to handle the shotgun .... *Lord
Walsingham (The Badminton Library, 1889).*

I know a good many pigeon shooters and find them, like
coarse fishermen, patient, resourceful, practical, down-to-earth

and, by and large, good shots. Those in whom these qualities are not well-developed will be unlikely to make the grade but will take up more congenial activities where success is more predictable . . . . *John Humphreys (Shooting Pigeons, 1988).*

The wood pigeon can present one of the hardest shots in all shooting. This is the bird who has decided to drop straight in, usually in windy conditions, from a great height. This bird makes the most of his variable geometry, closes his wings until they are little more than the size of vanes on a paper dart and slides down the wind, almost vertically, as fast as a high-speed lift. If you can kill him once in three shots you are doing extremely well. I know a good many good game shots who affect to despise pigeons. Truly, they have no idea what they are missing where pigeons are concerned, and where pigeons are concerned I've seen them do that, too . . . . *Colin Willock (The New ABC of Shooting, 1994).*

The wood pigeon is by nature a voracious bird, admittedly of handsome carriage and pigmented with a bit of real blue out of the sky, but a real villain of the worst order . . . . *Max Baker (Sport with Wood Pigeons, 1934).*

I

The Wood Pigeon and the British Countryside

CASUAL observers of the subject of this book may perhaps wonder why the bird is called 'wood pigeon'. Driving along in a car or looking out of a train window, the bird may be seen soaring into open fields, often to join large flocks already on the ground. In cities, if you notice it at all among the feral pigeons, you will see it strutting, like some overweight self-important civic dignitary, as it feeds on the clovers among the grass in parks and quiet squares.

Yet the bird *is* accurately and properly named. Its almost monotone grey plumage is that of a woodland species. If it lived and nested on the ground, it would be cryptically coloured like the partridge or the hen pheasant. Alarm it, as any shooter knows, and it heads back to the shelter of the trees. It nests in trees, except in rare habitats such as the Orkneys where trees are not readily available, and it certainly spends the night in trees. It uses bare trees as look-out points to see if the coast is clear before it descends to feed. Often, it prefers to flight to and from feeding grounds along the edge of woods and over shelter belts and even hedges, presumably because it feels most secure when tree cover is close at hand.

Though not a great deal is known about the wood pigeon's arrival in Britain it seems safe to assume that it only moved in when trees had already colonised the landscape. During the Pleistocene, the age which covers the last three million years, Europe underwent four major ice ages. Until around 8,000 years ago, deciduous woodland occured mainly in the Mediterranean region, in countries like Spain, Italy and Greece though it obtained a foothold in Britain during the interglacial periods. Wood pigeons almost certainly existed in these early deciduous forests. Then, as the ice made its last retreat, the trees advanced. Oak came to Britain about 4,000 years ago and beech followed about a thousand years later.

Stone Age man must have been familiar with the wood pigeon, though as a comparative rarity. The bird fed largely in the forests, in the treetops in spring on florets and buds; in the early autumn on berries; in November on beechmast and acorns—much as it does today, to the frustration of the pigeon shooter who finds acorn-gorging, beechmast-guzzling wood pigeon difficult if not impossible to decoy. In between, the birds would have supplemented their diet with clover, grassland weeds such as charlock and chickweed and fat hen, the last of which early man used as a vegetable as well as a substitute for grain. I doubt if the wood pigeon was present in sufficient numbers to damage neolithic man's modest harvest. Fat hen, if it was anything like as intrusive as it is today, must have been in ample supply.

Until two hundred years ago, it is likely that the wood pigeon population of these islands remained static. The bird may even have been something of a rarity. There are practically no specific references to it in early writings. Plenty about doves and tame pigeons but few about the wood pigeon.

An Old English dictionary compiled just before the Norman Conquest and edited by Wulcker in 1844 does mention 'cucote' and 'cowscott'. This probably meant wood pigeon. Both are close enough to one old country name for the bird still in use today, 'cushat' or 'cushy-doo', presumably of onomatopoeic origin associated with its song.

Early cookery books can usually be relied on to come up with some reference to almost any wild animal that was remotely edible. Where pigeons are concerned, such references as exist always refer to tame or dovecot pigeons for the very good reason that wild wood pigeons were not only scarce but almost impossible to harvest without a gun, whereas there were plenty of pigeons bred specially for the table. Even the industrious Dame Juliana Berners, who covered field sports and their prey extensively in 1460 in her *Boke of St Albans*, failed to include the wood pigeon. We have to wait until 1678 before the naturalist writer Francis

Willughby gave anything like an accurate description of the bird which he names *Palumbus targuatus.* 'These birds,' he wrote, 'in winter-time company together and fly in flocks; they build in trees, making their nests of a few sticks and straws. They feed upon acorns and also upon corn and ivy and holly berries.' It is a description you can hardly fault and it is certainly that of a bird that was still predominantly a woodland dweller.

The wood pigeon was still waiting for its big chance—the development of agriculture and particularly of arable farming—but it had to wait until the middle of the nineteenth century.

Before Tudor times, farming did little to favour the expansion of the species. Fields were cultivated as commonly-held strips, sown with wheat and rye in the autumn and with a spring sowing of oats and barley the following year. All the villagers' cattle were grazed on the stubbles after harvest. In the third year the land was left fallow and ploughed a couple of times. Apart from a few spilled grains when the corn ripened and those foraged round the feet of the grazing cattle after harvest, there was little here for the wood pigeon. No doubt, as the harvest ripened, the commoners took good care that the birds had little chance to deplete their precious and all-too-slender crops.

The old open-field system was bound to go, as a growing human population needed more food. Common grazing rights of the feudal system had given the farmers no chance to improve their harvests. The Enclosures, often bitterly resented and contested, followed. From 1760 until 1815, 1,800 Acts of Parliament were passed to enclose fields and meadows putting them into the hands of the landowners. The wood pigeon was not slow to take advantage of this new summer food supply. Even so, the bird needed a guaranteed source of winter food if it was significantly to increase in numbers. The abolition of common grazing soon provided this source. Now that there were no commoners' cattle and sheep to clean up the stubbles, farmers began to plant turnips on the ground that would formerly have lain fallow. Before long, they were undersowing their spring corn with clover. In hard weather, the wood pigeons found the turnips—just as they do today.

7

Even in snow two or three inches deep, the green tops of the root vegetables are still accessible to them. But it was the increasing amount of nitrogen-rich clover that gave the wood pigeon the final boost it needed.

Inevitably, the wood pigeon's expansion did not occur evenly throughout agricultural Britain. This is not surprising. The wood pigeon is the number one avian opportunist. The opportunities it looks for are basically two, and they are closely associated—an all-the-year-round supply of food within easy range of woods suitable for nesting and roosting. Where these occurred the birds thrived increasingly at the expense of the farmer.

There *are* one or two surprises in the pattern of expansion. The area of Hampshire, around Longparish, in which Colonel Peter Hawker lived in sporting splendour during the first half of the nineteenth century is today what might be described as prime pigeon country. Hawker, sometimes called 'the father of sporting shooting', shot everything that moved, including, so it is said, bats flying out of a burning barn. It is a dead certainty that if wood pigeon had been present in any numbers at Longparish he would have added them to the bag.

The Colonel kept complete records from 1802, when he was sixteen years old, until his death in 1853. The totals to his own flintlock gun recorded in his game books for this half century (excluding great numbers of wildfowl mostly shot with a punt-gun) are as follows: partridges, 7,035; pheasants, 575; blackcock, 11; grouse, 16; landrails, 56; quails, 58; *wood pigeons*, 20; turtle doves, 7; stock doves, 1; hares, 631; rabbits, 318.

In other words, the Colonel, who was not slow to draw a bead on anything flying or running, accounted for a wood pigeon slightly less than once every two years. Even if he regarded the pigeon, as do many game shooters today, as an occasional quarry met with when walking up other game, he would surely have scored more frequently if the birds had been present on his estate beside the River Test in any numbers. The only conclusion can be that they weren't! A part of the country that is now a pigeon paradise, was virtually barren. Why? Possibly because much of it was still devoted to grazing sheep rather than growing corn.

During the same period, and at somewhere close to the extreme range of the bird in the British Isles, the wood pigeon population exploded. In the early 1800s, the species enjoyed a boom in the grain-growing areas of central and eastern Scotland. By 1860 the birds were so plentiful in East Lothian that men with guns had to be posted in the harvest fields, not to shoot pigeons but simply to scare them off. Half a century earlier, in the same district, a single pair of nesting woodies had been talked about as a great rarity. So fast did the birds multiply, thanks to the new combination of grain, turnips and clover, that by 1862 the United East Lothian Agricultural Society put a price of one penny for each wood pigeon's head delivered. In the next eight years, 130,440 heads were turned in for this reward. A few years later, the Central Banffshire Farmers Club fought its own infestation, destroying 15,194 eggs, 1,603 juveniles and 3,733 adults.

The agricultural revolution marched side by side with the industrial revolution. The factory workers had to be fed so that their labour might in turn feed Britain's growing manufacturing prosperity. Townshend of Rainham and Coke of Holkham in Norfolk were the leaders of this revolution in farming thought and practice. They pioneered the rotation of crops and improved breeds of livestock which could now be overwintered thanks to the growing of winter roots instead of being slaughtered in the autumn. Townshend was not called 'Turnip' Townshend for nothing. If his and Coke's revolutionary agricultural ideas fed the workers they also indirectly fed the wood pigeon. And they made landowners and their tenant farmers who adopted their agricultural policies rich and secure.

Though it was plain that the wood pigeon was capable of enormous agricultural damage, not everyone saw its influence as entirely destructive. Charles St John in his *Wildsport of the Highlands* seeks to persuade a farmer that the pigeon is doing him a good turn:

An immense flock of wood pigeons busily at work in a field of young clover were really his benefactors. No amount of human labour and search could have collected on the same ground at that time of the year, as much of wild mustard and ragwort seeds as was consumed by these five or six hundred wood pigeons daily for two or three weeks together. Indeed during the whole of the summer and spring and a considerable part of the winter all pigeons feed actively on the seeds of wild plants.

St John does not record the reply but as the farmer's clover was suffering at the same or even greater rate as the weed seeds, I imagine that he wasn't too impressed by this argument.

As farming methods altered, and acres of arable in spring and summer and roots and clover in autumn and winter increased, so the wood pigeon expanded to take advantage of the bonanza. Nature, as is well documented, deplores a vacuum. If you could not exactly describe the new agriculture as a vacuum it was, at least, a magnificent opportunity for any creature disposed and able to exploit it. The wood pigeon filled this vacuum, or perhaps niche, to perfection. Throughout the nineteenth and twentieth centuries, the pigeon population not only increased but vastly extended its range, even into the suburbs and cities and to such almost treeless habitats as the Scottish islands as far north as the Orkneys.

Two world wars also proved to be to the birds' advantage. After the first, the need to grow timber to replace trees felled between 1914 and 1918 created new forest nesting habitats. During the second, the urgency of growing home-produced food to save Britain from starvation by the U-boat blockade provided new sources of pigeon fodder on practically every tillable acre in the land. On the minus side, both wars saw an increase in predators of the wood pigeon since there were no keepers to keep down the 'vermin'. No doubt the wood pigeon suffered an unusual number of casualties from nest-raiders and from birds of prey, for which, prior to the 1950s, keepers did not have the same respect nor the laws of protection their present force. But the wood pigeon was more than able to replace any gaps in its ranks, many times over.

Until the research programmes described in the introduction to this book are complete, and maybe not even then, no one, scientist or layman, can give more than an educated guess at the numbers of wood pigeon in Great

Britain. A very conservative estimate might be 'around fifteen million', or, to put it another way, nearly 8,000 tons of delectable flesh flying around the countryside eating many thousands of pounds worth of farm produce every day. For the foreseeable future, at least, the British countryside seems certain to provide the wood pigeon with everything it can possibly wish.

2

The Wood Pigeon and its Relations

THE wood pigeon is a delightful, handsome, highly-edible, strong-flying and at times almost aerobatic bird. Its breeding range is from central Scandinavia to about 65 degrees north, south to the northern Mediterranean coast, the Balaerics and Cyprus, eastward to the Black Sea, central Russia and Siberia. Very similar sub-species breed in Morocco, Tunisia and Algeria. But the largest concentration is within Great Britain. This population, of certainly fifteen million birds and maybe as many as twenty million, is sedentary with little, if any, migration to or from Europe.

The wood pigeon's *roo-coo-cooing* song is as much the sound of the British summer as that of the cuckoo. Tennyson's 'moan of doves in the immemorial elms' might almost have been written about *Columba palumbus*, although it is more likely that the poet had tame doves in mind. These days, no thanks to Dutch elm disease, Tennyson might have had to chose another tree species to grace his famous and evocative line. Elms, alas, are far from immemorial. Fortunately, the wood pigeon is. The wood pigeon's song has given rise to a series of country nicknames. In Scotland, it is sometimes called 'cushat', which may be onomatopoeic but which the Oxford English Dictionary says comes from 'the Old English, *cuscute*, origin unknown'. In *Rokeby*, Walter Scott refers to 'the cushat's murmur hoarse'. Alternatives are 'cushy-doo' or simply 'doo' which plainly hark back to its song. The label 'ring dove' needs no explanation. The Germans have the same word *ringeltaube* and Swiss *ringduva*. But what do you make of *quist*, or *queest* often heard in Wales and along the Welsh border? Even harder to place is *queert*.

It is impossible to confuse the wood pigeon with any of its relatives found in Great Britain. It is a large bird, about sixteen inches in length. In first-class condition, it weights at least a pound. Many game dealers, through whose hands great numbers of these birds pass, usually won't accept birds below that weight.

The upper parts of the body are blue-grey, the upper surfaces of the wings a darker grey. The tips of the primaries and tail feathers are black. The underside of the tail coverts show a broad black band and above that a white band. On the sides of the neck are pure white patches which give it the name ring dove, although these white marks don't meet to form a complete collar. The sides of the neck are iridescent, a mixture of purple and green, and play a part in display.

But it is the breast colouring which so perfectly sets the bird off. The breast is blush pink which merges into pale grey on the belly. The wings have a broad white band to match the half collar of the neck. Both these white surfaces give important signals. The wing markings reveal, as the bird planes in to land, that it has found a worthwhile source of food. The neck ring possibly serves the same purpose, though when the head is raised in alarm it seems likely that this acts as a warning signal to birds feeding around it or in the air about to join the feeding flock.

The coral-pink legs provide a nice finishing touch to the whole ensemble, while the eye with is straw-coloured, pear-shaped iris gives the wood pigeon a most sagacious expression. If this is an anthropomorphic observation then I make no apology. About its own business of being a wood pigeon, and therefore a great opportunist and survivor, the bird most certainly *is* sagacious.

Quite apart from any wisdom mirrored in that knowing eye, the eye itself is amazingly acute. The bird is certainly able to see and read unwelcome or dangerous signals—such as the movement of the human face, or arm, particularly if the latter is holding a shotgun—at ranges of up to half a mile! I have a private though unscientific suspicion that monocular vision allows the bird to glimpse objects, or at least movement, when it has flown past. In other words it is partly able to see backwards.

R.K. Murton summed up the wood pigeon's appearance with a sharpness of appreciation born of a career studying his subject.

'The plumage,' he wrote, 'has a sort of bloom which gives the bird a bright appearance.' No description could be more apt.

It is said that males are bigger than females, though it would be a lucky guess on most people's part if they succeeded in telling the sexes apart by this criterion. There is no doubt about juveniles, however. They are slimmer and not so well developed in the first free-flying months of their life. They are far less cautions and they lack the white neck rings (but not the white wing bars) and the iridescent neck of the adults. The beak, as in most young birds, is softer and more flexible, and there are likely to be a number of incompletely moulted feathers, especially on the wings. Many of the feathers will have a brownish tip. These young birds, which are on the wing in late summer and early autumn, will not acquire the full adult livery until well into the new year.

Plumage variations are fairly rare. I have never come across a completely white, let alone an albino, wood pigeon which would, of course, have to have a pink eye to qualify. But I have shot a couple of 'isabelline' birds which are a dirty grey in colour. People to whom I have mentioned this are puzzled by the term. I was, too, until that great ornithologist and wildfowler the late Jeffery Harrison enlightened me. The word is said to come from Isabella of Spain, whose armies were besieging Ostend. She was wearing a white dress at the time and swore that she would not change her apparel until her forces were triumphant. Happily, her armies prevailed, but it took years! By the time victory was hers, the dress was a sad shade of off-white. It was, in fact, 'isabelline'. But others have it that the word was already in use by that time.

The wood pigeon has relatives in practically every country in the world, though it has many more relations in the Old World than the New. Pigeons and doves—there really is no difference except perhaps that the smaller members of the family are usually referred to as doves— belong to the order *Columbiformes* and the sub-order *Columbae*. There are somewhere around three hundred species divided into fifty genera. Ornithologists seem unable to make up their minds about the exact totals. Most species occur in tropical and subtropical countries with more than half the world's species in the Indo–Malayan and Australasian regions.

The range of colouration and size is immense. Birds like the Namaqua dove of southern Africa are little bigger than a wagtail. The crowned pigeon of New Guinea is about the size of a Rhode Island Red, although it is in fact blue. I observed a tiny example of pigeon variation, while writing this chapter, on the small island of Antigua in the Eastern Caribbean. Three species lived around the hut beside a bird lagoon at Galley Bay in which my wife and I were staying. They ranged from the quail-sized common ground dove (*Columbina passerina*)—one of the neatest little members of the family I have had the good fortune to meet—through the elegant, reddish-brown Zenaida dove (*Zenaida aurita*)—a bird with a monotonous off-key single note call—to the truly noble white-crowned pigeon (*Columba leucocephala*), a slate-grey bird with iridescent slanting lines on its neck and a pronounced white topknot. Incidentally, these three species, which occur on other islands in the Antilles, illustrate the ornithologist's tendency to classify the larger species as pigeons and the lesser ones as doves. The white-crowned pigeon could nearly match the homely wood pigeon in size and portliness. Antigua boasted five dove species in all, though I never caught up with the red-necked pigeon (*Columba squamosa*) and the bridled quail dove (*Geotrygon mystacea*).

Despite their adaptability, pigeon species are not immune from extinction. Five have disappeared in the last three hundred years—which as extinction goes these days is not too bad a record. The most dramatic total disappearance of all took place in America, in Cincinnati Zoo to be exact, at precisely 1 pm on 1 September, 1914. A century before, North America had been home to many billions of passenger pigeons. Nobody has recorded exactly how many, though John James Audubon, the great bird artist of nineteenth-century America, reckoned that in 1813 he personally watched a total of a billion of these long-tailed pigeons fly over on migration. One hundred years later, the last survivor died in captivity. Wholesale slaughter for market and destruction of the forests had been jointly responsible.

Our own wood pigeon exists in nothing like these numbers. Nevertheless, with a probable wood pigeon population of over fifteen million, distributed by no means evenly throughout a comparatively small island, Britain's wood pigeon may well be running a fair second to the passenger pigeon in the density stakes. And at present, the wood pigeon is certainly in no danger of following the exit marked 'extinction'; quite the contrary. All the same, the lesson of the passenger pigeon is writ clear. We should be glad that the situation is being scientifically monitored.

They are an interesting lot, the wood pigeon's relatives. The *Columbiformes* include the sandgrouse and once included the flightless dodo of Mauritius and the equally grounded solitaire of Reunion and Rodriguez. The dodo became extinct in 1681 and the solitaire in 1791.

All *Columbiformes* have a unique way of drinking. Where other birds take a sip of water and tilt back their heads to swallow, pigeons and sandgrouse can immerse their beaks and suck directly as if through a straw, though it has to be added that sandgrouse can drink using both methods. Next time you get a chance, watch a wood pigeon suck up water at a garden pond or perhaps a cattle trough.

I cannot let any mention of sandgrouse, which are really a sort of combination of game bird and pigeon, pass without describing another unique way these fascinating birds use water. I once watched an estimated 50,000 chestnut-bellied sandgrouse (the estimate was world bird expert Leslie Brown's rather than mine) fly in from the desert to drink at a small sandy beach on a river in the Ethiopian Rift Valley. The birds came in a continuous noisy stream. You could hear the chortle of the flocks a mile or more away in the desert, long before the first cloud of birds became visible.

The first parties thronged on to the little beach, more and more landing and pressing forward from behind all the time. The leaders walked down to the river for their day's water supply. Most sucked after the manner of their kind. A few sipped and tilted. What was most interesting though was to watch the male birds fluff out their breast feathers and dip them in the stream. When they took off you could see their breasts swollen with the water trapped in their specially adapted feathers. They were carrying this water back to their young in the nests miles away in the open desert. Only the males can do this. All the 50,000 birds had come, drunk and flown back inside six minutes. I've never seen a bird spectacle to equal it. It took place five days in succession and then stopped as if a switch had been turned off. The sandgrouse had found somewhere else to drink.

The *Columbiformes* also have a special adaptation when it comes to feeding their young. They have a sac-like pocket in the oesophagus in which they store food in order to regurgitate it to their chicks.

The wood pigeon can go one better than that, however. The *Columba*, the genus to which the wood pigeon belongs, produce a special secretion on the walls of the crop, often called 'pigeon's milk' and not so far removed in composition from mammalian milk. Cells in the crop of a brooding pigeon become glandular and fill with a creamy, cheese-like substance. When the cells are full, this substance oozes out and fills the crop from which it is regurgitated to the young birds. Many years ago and the first time I cleaned a wood pigeon in this condition I was ignorant enough to think that it had a cancerous growth in its crop.

'Pigeon's milk' does, in fact, differ quite considerably from mammal's milk. Research (J. Needham, 1942) shows that it is composed of water, protein, fat and various salts high in sodium. It contains no carbohydrate but is rich in vitamins A, B and B2. Unlike mammal's milk it contains no calcium. To produce this milk is a considerable strain on the adult's bodily reserves. It gives the young the advantage of being more-or-less independant of food gathered by the parents from the countryside during the first few days of nestling life.

Now for the wood pigeon's relatives that either reside in, or visit, Great Britain. Perhaps we should begin with the stock dove (*Columba oenas*) if only for the reason that it consorts with the wood pigeon, feeds on much the same sort of farmland and will come in to decoys set out by the pigeon shooter to entice the wood pigeon. Until 1981, the shooter could take advantage of this gullibility, but the Wildlife and

Countryside Act of that year, for reasons best known to our law-makers but beyond the understanding of most countrymen, gave the stock dove protection.

When I have questioned this item of apparently daft legislation with ornithologists, they have told me that I only see the picture from my own neck of the woods, where there appears to be a plethora of stock doves. Nationwide, they tell me, the prospects for the stock dove are by no means so healthy. If these experts are right, then obviously we cannot quarrel with the provisions of the Wildlife and Countryside Act but I beg leave to doubt the soundness of this piece of legislation. The *New Atlas of Breeding Birds* published in 1993 reported, 'The current population levels measured by the common bird census are about double those at the time of the 1968–72 Atlas.' Is there really justification for protection?

Of course, pigeon shooters are only human, and may therefore occasionally make a mistake in identifying the neat little stock dove over their decoys. Ignorance of the law, or failure to identify correctly, is, however, no excuse. It is possible that a genuine mistake may be excused or not even be noticed. But it is as well to remember that the law is the law and that even in the middle of a twenty-acre barley stubble you can never be sure that you are not being observed through the binoculars of a bird-watcher or of a member of an anti-fieldsports organisation. Terrible is the wrath of birders, especially the sleuths of the Royal Society for the Protection of Birds. Pigeon shooters beware. There really is no excuse for breaking the law or, for that matter, failing to identify the stock dove correctly.

Bird-watchers sometimes use an excellent term to describe the general appearance of a bird, even when seen in flight and at a distance. The word is 'jizz'. The jizz of the stock dove as compared with that of its larger relative the wood pigeon is smaller and neater, and its head and neck are more tucked in to the body. Unlike the wood pigeon, the stock dove has not a scrap of white on its entire plumage. Instead, the upper surfaces of each wing show two black marks, one in front of the other, though, of course, these can rarely be seen when the bird is flying. The plumage is darker than that of the wood pigeon and the neck has a purplish hue that is slightly iridescent. The flight sometimes seems faster and more evasive than that of the wood pigeon, though this, admittedly, is often an illusion promoted by lack of size and speed of wing. (For instance, a teal always seems to be flying faster than a mallard but almost certainly is not.)

Novice shooters may find the following point a further help in identifying their quarry: stock doves seldom approach decoys in more than pairs. In the days when they were legal quarry, if one was shot, it was an even bet that its mate, or anyway companion, would come round again, often with fatal results, to find out what had happened to its 'wing-man'. In those days shooters seldom failed to take advantage of this faithfulness unto death. Stock doves were delicious eating. Even in winter, when many wood pigeons are in poor condition, the stock dove is usually plump and well fed. Stock doves, which exist largely on a diet of seeds, always seem to be able to find a supply of these, largely from weeds, right through the hardest weather.

Prior to the 1981 Act, a friend who shot pigeons professionally had an excellent market for stock doves. He sold them to a Bond Street hotel, a haunt of visiting Americans, where, thanks to their diminutive size, they were put on the menu as 'squab' (tender young pigeon).

In throwing doubt in an earlier paragraph on the wisdom or ornithological knowledge of our law-makers, I had in mind that the stock dove does a certain, even if small, amount of agricultural damage and yet earned protection. I have, for example, often found stock dove crops packed full of useful seeds such as radish and usually a modicum of corn although I believe that the species has little adverse affect upon farming. This might be a good enough reason for protecting it, had not the same Act put the smaller collared dove (*Streptopelia decaocto*) on the list of birds that may legitimately be shot. The poor little collared dove does even less damage and is so small that few shooters are willing to use powder and shot to take advantage of the provision of the 1981 Act. The law in the case of these two birds does seem to be, if not actually an ass, then highly inconsistent.

Since I have already mentioned the collared dove I will deal with it next. In the late 1950s I remember becoming highly excited when I spotted a dove with a tail like a parakeet sitting on a telephone wire at a roundabout outside Devizes. It was the first collared dove I had seen. It had long been said that these invaders from Eastern Europe were on their way to take over Britain. Now here was one of their advance scouts. In the next decade every suburban garden had a pair or more of collared doves. Spring and summer mornings were rendered discordant by their courtship songs which might be compared to a wood pigeon with a severe attack of laryngitis. It is anything but soothing let alone sleep-inducing.

They are undeniably pretty birds with a narrow black half collar worn at the back of the neck and an overall plumage of pale brown. The rear half of the underside of the tail is white.

Though collared doves flock in large numbers in the autumn to capitalise on any loose harvest grain they can find around barns and silos, they are more a nuisance than an agricultural menace. Perhaps the worst thing they do, apart from pecking away at vegetable patches, is to befoul the areas they frequent. They will often overfly decoys but seldom pitch in amongst them. I can vouch for the fact that they are good eating, though you need quite a number to make a casserole. Their breasts, lightly grilled on toast, can prove a gourmet dish.

As explained previously, few pigeon shooters think they are worth a cartridge. I did on one occasion watch a famous game shot account for over sixty in an hour and a half when the birds were flighting out of a wood in a high wind. They were tricky shooting even for this master. His average, he confessed, was slightly worse than two cartridges per bird.

The collared dove is sometimes called the ringed turtle dove. The true turtle dove (*Streptopelia turtur*) is fully protected. It is easily distinguished from that invader from the East, the collared dove. It is more slender, has an overall rufous appearance and a smoothly-rounded, white-tipped tail. It is a summer migrant from southern Europe, and its song, a melodious purring coo is 'the voice of the turtle' celebrated in 'The Song of Solomon'. It has a quick, flicking flight and cannot possibly be mistaken even for a collared dove.

The last of the four wild pigeons of Britain has been protected since 1981. It is confined to a very limited, though largely inaccessible, habitat—tall cliffs, usually sea cliffs. The blue rock dove (*Columba livia*) has an honoured place in the ornithological history of these islands since it is the un-doubted ancestor of all our domestic pigeons be they fantails, tumblers, dovecot pigeons, town ferals or high-bred racers. Its descendants come in many colours, including chequered red. It is highly likely that some of these domestic offshoots have at times bred back into the wild rock dove stock.

The rock dove is about the same size as the stock dove, though confusion is never likely to arise as they will seldom be found in the same habitat, although blue rocks occasionally come inland to feed in wood pigeon habitat. The bird has two broad black bands right across the wing secondary feathers and white beneath the wing surfaces. The tail has a black band at its trailing edge. The overall colour is blue-grey with a glossy sheen and lilac in the neck. In flight, it usually keeps lower and is faster than the wood pigeon. It has probably developed these flight patterns to counter one of its main predators, the peregrine falcon that occupies the cliff habitat with it. In the old days, before protection, the guns usually went afloat in a small boat at the foot of the cliffs.

Finally, a word about the rock dove's tame descendants. These are the feral pigeons seen in vast numbers in the centre of cities and usually causing a great nuisance with their droppings. The decoy shooter frequently meets them in large numbers. They can, of course, be legally shot as crop raiders but great care should be used. A large pack of pigeons flying together and in a purposeful and organised fashion should always be left alone. They may well be racers, or the occupants of a pigeon loft turned out for exercise. In both cases, they will be the valued and highly-valuable property of some pigeon enthusiast. Odd, persistant ferals in small numbers who come in to decoys are more likely to be 'escapes', tame birds gone wild, and perfectly legal quarry if you are so minded. Some look rather like stock doves but they can usually be identified by the high dihedral angle at which they raise their wings when soaring. To the decoy expert they are a serious nuisance, as their presence seems to discourage the genuine wild article. The best thing, perhaps, is simply to scare them off. They are quite good eating but there is some doubt as to the wisdom of making use of them in the kitchen though they should be safe enough if thoroughly cooked. There is a suspicion that some of these birds may carry or spread disease. If so, it is more likely to be a lung infection caused by their droppings where concentrations of these birds roost. If you have ferrets to feed you may, however, feel justified in pulling the trigger. When all is said and done, from a farming, sporting and culinary point of view, it is the wood pigeon that is the true, legitimate and only worthwhile quarry.

3

The Natural History of the Wood Pigeon

THE total number of hours I have spent in the past thirty years sitting in pigeon hides or standing in roosting woods at dusk numbers many thousand. Some of that time I have spent actually shooting, or, anyway shooting at, pigeons. At least half the time has been passed *not* shooting, for, on balance, wood pigeons only oblige in about seventy-five per cent of the time spent in trying to outwit them. I do not regret a single minute of it. Anglers have a saying to the effect that 'time spent in fishing shall not be counted among the total of your days'. Well, I feel a bit like that about pigeon shooting. In a hide you are, if you have built and sited it properly, by definition, hidden. You become as much part of the countryside as the hawthorn hedge, the muddy plough or the budding oak. You are in an unrivalled position to observe the things that go on around you and not least the wood pigeon. Even if the bird shuns your decoys *en route* to a more enticing feeding ground, you have ample opportunity to observe the species' comings and goings.

Amongst your equipment you will have, or should have, a pair of binoculars—an invaluable pigeon shooter's aid. With these, when not otherwise engaged, you can watch the pair on the edge of a distant wood courting, displaying, building a nest or a male patrolling his territory with soaring flight and clap of wing which say to rivals, 'this is my patch. Keep off!'

In time, the keen pigeon shooter builds up, as I have done, an extensive though perhaps not very expert knowledge of his quarry's natural history. I make no pretence of approaching the subject scientifically or with expert ornithological knowledge. For that I must turn to the scientists. And so here and now I freely acknowledge my debt to R.K. Murton (*The Wood Pigeon*, Collins New Naturalist), M.K. Colquhoun (*The Wood Pigeon in Britain*, HMSO), Stanley Cramp (*Territorial and other Behaviour of the Wood Pigeon*, Bird Study 5:55-66), Dr Ian Inglis who carries on Dr Murton's work at the study area at Carlton in Cambridgeshire, and many more dedicated and knowledgeable workers in this field. Their studies and observations have told us practically everything we know about the bird. I am only an enthusiastic lay observer.

One of the problems facing those who would like to give the wood pigeon a close season would be to decide exactly where to place the fence months. Wood pigeons have been known to rear their young in every month of the year. A further complication is a geographical one: birds further north run to a different and later schedule. The availability of the right kind of food, which means a cropping plan favourable to the bird, plays a large part in breeding success.

It seems safe to say that breeding really starts in early March and sometimes late February. It is almost certainly the length and quality of increasing daylight that tells the birds' gonads that it is time to start thinking of the next generation. The males get the message about a fortnight before their prospective mates. There is a good reason for this. Before anything else can happen, the male birds have to claim and stake out a territory.

At first, not all the males in a flock do this and even those that do so don't spend the whole day claim-staking. These early territorial males start soon after dawn, moving down from the treetops, where they have roosted with other members of the flock, to the lower levels of the tree canopy. There they serenade the countryside with a melodious if monotonous song which ornithologists write down as the *coo-cooo-cooo-co-co* note. This song, in fact, is very far from a serenade. It is a warning to other wood pigeons to keep their distance.

When the main flock quits the roost for the feeding grounds, these males leave with them or sometimes shortly after. The woods are then bare of pigeons for the rest of the day. In March and early April, daylight hours are still short and as much feeding as possible must be crammed into the time available.

When the birds return to roost in the evening, the territorial males take up where they left off. As the days lengthen, these males become more aggressive during the morning and evening territory proclaiming sessions until they have succeeded in persuading rivals that it is unwise to try to sleep in their preserves. Not all the birds in a flock will eventually breed in the roosting woods. Some will choose hedges and small isolated copses. These males leave the wood early in the morning and go through the claim-staking rituals in their selected hedge or tree but return to the main roost at night.

By April almost the whole adult population is in breeding condition, though first-year birds will probably not reach this pitch until July. The balance between feeding hours and time spent in the territories changes in favour of the latter. Provided they can get sufficient food, the pigeons spend more and more time in their territories. The large feeding flocks seen on the fields in February and March are breaking up.

For the pigeon shooter this is not necessarily a bad thing. Big flocks that scare off *en masse* at a single shot are the devil to come to terms with. A steady trickle of birds flying in to the decoys throughout the day is much more productive. So, spring pigeon decoyers who can find birds feeding steadily and in small parties on newly-drilled corn or peas may well be in for a bonanza.

May can prove far less satisfactory. The pigeons spend more and more hours in the treetops, feeding on buds and florets, especially from beech and ash. These birds are, in fact, behaving very much like the wood pigeons of medieval times described earlier, in other words as *wood* pigeons. The woodlands are now dreamy with the sounds of pigeon cooing, or so it seems to the human ear. Actually, it is far from a dream for the songsters. Territorial activity is at its height, as males attempt to drive off rivals. If song fails, then physical force, or at least threat of force, may be used. A threatening male stands with head raised, neck stretched out, wings and back plumage raised, all devices intended to make the displaying bird look bigger and more menacing. It is rather like a dog raising its hackles. If the hint is not taken, the territory owner sometimes flies at his rival or alights close by and repeats the display, chasing his enemy around the territory until he disappears to try his luck elsewhere. If the intruder stands his ground, then an actual 'punch-up' may take place, the birds sitting side by side nodding and flicking their wings at each other.

In extreme cases, they will peck and strike blows with the wings that can sometimes knock a rival off his branch. I have watched fights like this in the three tall oaks in my garden on summer evenings. On occasions, the battle has lasted for more than an hour with the contestants shifting from tree to tree and sometimes on to the roof of the house.

The territorial display with which pigeon shooters will be most familiar, simply because it often takes place in the open, is the soaring flight of the male ending in a stall and accompanied by a sharp clap of the wings. Many people believe this is produced by the raised wings hitting each other. Apparently, the clap occurs on the down-stroke with the pinions acting rather like the crack of a whip, though I would certainly like to see the issue settled on super-slow-motion film. Although I once wrote and produced a film on wood pigeons in the *Survival* series of TV natural history documentaries, we never succeeded in getting the wing-clap shot in slow motion.

While the males establish territories, the females are coming to breeding pitch. Unmated females venture into the males' territories. If they are lucky, and they almost invariably are, their submissive attitude will provoke a bowing display from the male. Pigeons can only tell the sex of another pigeon by its behaviour and displays. Those who are not familiar with wood pigeons will at least have seen males bowing in courtship among city and dovecot pigeons.

The phrase applied to human courtship in former times, 'billing and cooing', obviously comes directly from the observation of tame or dovecot birds. The bowing, with head lowered and tail raised and fanned out, is accompanied by a courtship song, translated by those with a quick enough ear as *co-roo-co-co-co-coo*. The billing comes later. At first, when solicited by bowing and song, the female often flies away.

The reason she does so is not so much because she is coy but because the bowing display by the male has aggressive overtones. At this stage the female isn't quite sure whether sex or aggression is uppermost in her swain's mind.

Eventually, the female decides that sex is really what the male bird is thinking about. She gradually approaches closer to him. The start of a pair bond is being formed. The next stage is known as 'nest-calling'.

Many bird displays are ritualised forms of activities associated with breeding. Nest-calling displays are almost certainly one of these. They are performed at the same time as the males—but occasionally the females—give the nest-calling song (translated by the ornithologists as *oooo-aaarh*). The bird pecks downward in the direction of his mate's breast while vibrating the wings and fanning his tail. R.J. Andrew theorises in *Ibis* (1961) that the wing movements are derived from the wing vibrations of hungry young asking to be fed. The pecking and tail-spreading (for balance?) resemble attitudes the wood pigeon strikes when collecting material for and building the nest. Taken together these displays are reassuring to the female.

Billing and cooing? So far there has been plenty of cooing. The billing comes now, at the stage when the pair bond has been firmly established. Billing consists of mutually gentle pecking and preening and generally takes place near the nest site that the male has selected. Caressing plays an important part in stimulating ovulation in the female.

The pair start to build as soon as they have agreed upon a nest site. If an old nest has been chosen, it will be cleaned out and simply strengthened with a few twigs. Both sexes collect nesting material from the ground or by breaking it off a growing plant or tree. A wood pigeon's bill is surprisingly powerful, and needs to be since much of its green leaf food has to be torn from the plant. One pigeon usually stays on site and weaves in the sticks as the partner delivers them.

All this time, caressing and singing goes on to further reinforce the pair-bond. A.J. Petersen (1955) demonstrated that a high level of certain chemicals within a bird's body—notably oestrogen and androgen—or, to put it another way, rapid ovular and testicular growth, was needed to initiate nest-building. The same applies to the onset of copulation.

Copulation is preceeded by an increase in billing in which the female usually takes the lead. The pair hold each other's bills, the female often inserting hers into the male's gape. In this courtship 'feeding', food is actually sometimes passed, the female imitating the begging posture of a nestling. Copulation seldom occurs on the nest but on a nearby branch. It lasts two or three seconds and is often repeated several times, separated by brief spells of billing and cooing.

No countryman will have any difficulty in recognising a wood pigeon's nest. It resembles an untidy pile of sticks about nine inches in diameter. The main 'girders' may be sticks a foot in length, while the lining is made of smaller and finer twigs and sometimes grass. First-time nests are often quite flimsy, so skeletal in fact that the eggs can on occasion be seen through the bottom.

The wood pigeon has definite preferences when it comes to choice of tree. Not surprisingly, early nesting birds show a preference for evergreens. Sitka spruce is more sought after than Norway spruce because its foliage is denser. Among deciduous species, hawthorn, hazel, blackthorn, elder and honeysuckle are seen as more highly desirable residences than ash, beech, elm or oak. Ivy is also favoured. Thickness of cover seems to be the key factor. The birds prefer to build within fifty feet of the edge of the wood rather than at its centre.

Most nests occur between five and twenty feet above the ground. In mature trees, in my own garden for instance, I have a wood pigeon nest some sixty feet up. This may be due to lack of cover—which is thickest in the upper canopy of the tree—but is more likely to be a reaction to disturbance by the house-owners, their dogs, grandchildren, guests and lawn-mowers. The same height phenomenon can be seen in city parks and no doubt for the same reason. City wood pigeons are sometimes forced by the same factors to make some very odd selections. When making a *Survival* film on wildlife in London, the cameraman, George Edwards, found and filmed a pair of wood pigeon that had nested and successfully reared young in an old-fashioned pavement lamp post!

Where nesting pressure is high and competition for sites intense, or in areas where trees are in short supply (the Orkneys for one), pigeons will nest on the ground—in hedge bottoms, beds of nettles and even in standing corn.

There is an old saying to describe human twins, one of whom is a boy, the other a girl, as 'a pigeon pair'. The saying arises, so far as I can trace, from the belief that pigeons, which normally lay two eggs, *invariably* produce one male and one female. I have come across this superstition, for it can be no more than that, quite recently among otherwise knowledgeable countrymen. It would be interesting to know what the actual sex ratio of the young is, but since adult pigeons can't tell male from female without the appropriate displays, I can see little hope of sexing nestlings, let alone enough young, to obtain a representative sample. What the effect would be on the wood pigeon population were this old wive's saying true gives rise to fascinating speculation. With most bird species, nature needs far fewer males than females, since one cock can fertilise an indefinite number of hens. But with a bird like the wood pigeon, with its elaborate courtship and joint rearing and feeding of the young, a more evenly-matched population of males and females may be nature's answer.

To return to the known facts . . . . The usual clutch is two eggs, though nests with one to four eggs have been known. It is likely that the three- and four-egg clutches are the result of more than one female laying in the same nest.

Before egg-laying there is a 'house-warming' period of up to a week when both birds sit on the empty nest. Egg-laying takes about two days. Pigeon eggs are nearly white and are horribly evident to patrolling jays and magpies. Both parents incubate, taking every possible care not to leave the eggs unguarded or uncovered.

When one bird relieves the other at the next, the change-over takes place on the nest or on a branch close enough to warn off any predator waiting its chance. Egg losses are biggest early in the year, probably because the parents find food harder to collect. There is therefore an urge for a hungry bird to leave the nest before its partner returns.

The eggs hatch in an average of seventeen days, the parents carrying the tell-tale white shells away from the nest. For three days the adults feed the squabs entirely on 'pigeon milk'. After this, they give them a mixture of milk and the food they are gathering for themselves. At four days, the nestlings' eyes open. At eight to ten days, the young are fed only twice a day by each parent. By then, the feathers are appearing.

The young remain in the nest for up to twenty-two days, getting fed less and less frequently, perhaps by only one of the parents. About this time, the adults begin courtship all over again, often building a new nest within a few yards of the first one and even laying a new clutch. It is not unusual for a pair to be running two nests, one with eggs in it and the other with nearly fledged young.

When the young leave the nest, they are still fed by their parents, probably for a week, though the actual time is not definitely established. At first, the youngsters stay within the family territory and may even return to the nest site to roost. Dr Murton recorded young in his study area in Cambridgeshire that strayed into other birds' territories and succeeded in begging food from strange adults.

The peak breeding season and production of young occurs between July and September with a high point in August. All animals produce young most successfully when food is most plentiful. This applies as much to the wood pigeon in Hertfordshire as to the wildebeeste on the Serengeti. Seventy per cent of the wood pigeon population do not begin to breed until the cereal crops of summer are ripening. Strangely, those birds that nest early in March and April have a better chance of success than the June nesters. This is probably because the food available in May and June—florets, buds, unripe corn—has poor nutritional value. At this time, up to fifty per cent of the young may die in the nest.

Though eggs are always at risk, young wood pigeons, except when a few days old, do not appear to suffer greatly from predation by corvids or even by squirrels. Possibly, this is because they can adopt a quite frightening threat posture, puffing out their feathers, inflating their crops and raising their wings at the same time hissing with air released from the crop.

Pigeon shooters can expect to see young over their decoys in increasing numbers from July onwards. If they are wise, those who may well sell their bag to a game dealer will reserve these juveniles for their own freezers. They are tender and quite delicious. Stupidly, though perhaps understandably because juveniles are smaller, game dealers are reluctant to buy the tender young birds.

There is no mistaking the juveniles. Though they have the white wing bars of the adults, they lack the white neck collar. I have surmised earlier that this white ring plays its part as a warning and maybe feeding signal to other birds in the area. There is no doubt, however, that the white neck is used in sexual display. The young birds won't be thinking of courtship until the following year. This could be the explanation of the absence of white ring, whereas the white wing bars will be used as a 'land-here-I've-found-food' signal and possibly even as a warning, from the outset.

The white ring may not appear until the following spring. The summer batch of young moult their juvenile plumage after six weeks, in October and November. At this stage, the brown-tipped 'baby feathers' disappear and the iridescent neck begins to show up. A hard winter, however, can stop the process, so that some young may go through the hard months in mixed plumage. When they start to moult again in February or March, they don't take up the feather growth where they left off. Instead, they begin the process of acquiring adult plumage all over again.

Though it *is* possible for a pair of wood pigeons to produce three broods in a year, very few do so. Dr Murton reckoned that to maintain the population (which, in 1959, he put at over five million) a pair of wood pigeons needed to rear 0.72 young 'because thirty-six out of every hundred adults die each year'. In 1957, national inquiries showed that the average production per pair was more like 2.4 young annually. A lot has altered since then, including, as we shall see, the winter food sources of the wood pigeon. That change is greatly to the birds' advantage. At the moment of writing, the wood pigeon appears to be more successful than ever, even though the production rate has fallen since Morton's

4

Wood Pigeon, Public Enemy

THE wood pigeon is the only bird in these islands that is a serious threat to agriculture. Bullfinches may attack the blossom in fruit-growing areas. Songbirds take their share of the nurseryman's raspberries and strawberries. But compared to the wood pigeon these are merely schoolboys scrumping apples. The wood pigeon feeds all year round on the best that the farmer and countryside can produce—cereals both when they are newly sown and when they have ripened, peas and beans likewise, brassicas, clover, and much more besides. Moreover, there are many millions of eager diners around to select from this extensive and expensive menu.

Delightful as the wood pigeon is to look upon; melodious as it may be, in small doses anyway, to hear in summer song; great sporting bird that it undoubtedly is; all these admirable qualities are outweighed a million times as far as the farmer is concerned by the damage it does to his crops.

In an earlier chapter we saw how damaging it was to the lowland farmers of Scotland as long ago as the middle of the nineteenth century. Since then, infestation by wood pigeon has become general except in hill country, with the highest populations living, breeding and feeding in the areas intensively cultivated for cereals and more recently sown with oilseed rape.

To get some idea of the scale and seriousness of the damage the bird causes, it helps to understand not only what the bird eats but *how* it eats. Apart from being a fascinating example of highly-successful adaptation in action, such knowledge is undoubtedly useful to the shooter who seeks consistently to outwit the wood pigeon.

Shooters who clean and dress their own birds—and I don't know any serious pigeon man who would do otherwise—are best acquainted with what the pigeon eats through the contents of its crop. From time to time letters appear in the sporting press reporting exceptional, even what the writers claim to be record, cropfuls, thus: two hundred peas, fifty acorns, ninety tic beans, three ounces of barley.

Anyone who has stood in a roosting wood on a cold evening in winter or early spring, and watched pigeon coming home to spend the night in the trees, will have noticed the bulge between head and breast. In this condition, the birds always remind me of a man who has stuffed a pillow under the front of a pale pink sweater. The 'bolster' consists of a crop stuffed with greenstuff. Without this vital storage organ the pigeon could not exist in Britain in anything like its present numbers.

In winter, and in hard weather especially, the wood pigeon relies on green food. Until a few years ago, this consisted of clovers, turnip tops and brassicas such as kale. Nowadays these winter foods have been largely supplanted by oilseed rape (*Brassica napus*). Oilseed rape was first brought to England in the seventeenth century by the Dutch engineers who drained the Fens. They planted it as a source of oil to lubricate the windmills they used as water pumps.

Animals that live entirely on green food have a problem to get enough nourishment from it, especially protein. Ruminants get round this by bolting large amounts of food and digesting it later—chewing the cud. Rabbits recycle the only partly-digested pellets they pass at night. To put it another way: they eat their food twice, or anyway one and a half times. In winter, when green-feeding, the wood pigeon solves the problem by having a crop that can expand like a balloon.

That flock of pigeons you see feeding on a field of rape are tearing off leaves and tucking them away far faster than they can digest them. The leaf fragments go into the crop where no digestion takes place. So the pigeons you watch coming home to roost with a bulge under their sweaters are going to digest their crop contents throughout the night. But for this storage organ, the wood pigeon would be unable to take advantage of the huge supply of winter food modern farming makes available to it.

Dr Murton's field studies at Carlton in the 1950s and 1960s still give us a very clear idea of how the wood pigeon feeds throughout the season. Starting at the beginning of the year, until the mass planting of rape began, the winter flocks relied largely on clovers to see them through until the spring. Now they switch their attention to young winter rape. In February and March many rape fields appear to have been well worked over with a ticket punch.

In winter, daylight hours are short—from 8 am to 4 pm— and the flocks spend up to ninety per cent of these gathering food. Murton worked out that on clover each pigeon ate or stored away up to 35,000 single items, usually leaf fragments, each day. About 4,000 of these remained undigested in the crop when the bird went to roost. The total is likely to be about the same on oilseed rape, though, because it is so readily available and does not have to be searched for, as does clover, the gathering process may take less time, leaving more for preening and resting.

As far as the shooter is concerned, these large rape-feeding flocks are easily spooked. There are invariably other rape fields to which they can move. At this time of year, the birds are concentrated into big flocks. Once shot off there is usually no neighbouring flock to replace them. At first sight, they look a tempting proposition. Experienced guns will know that (a) they probably won't decoy, (b) they are likely to disappear over the horizon after a dozen shots, and (c) if they stay that long, the reward for several hours work is unlikely to be more than a dozen birds, maybe only half that number!

Spring is a better time for both wood pigeon and shooter. Daylight is increasing. At first, spring drilling of corn, peas and spring rape—to which the farmer is increasingly turning— make food-gathering easy. Pigeons have more time for other activities. Some pairs start to nest and even rear young though without a high rate of success.

A slump follows the spring sowing period. In May and June, to the shooter's chagrin, wood pigeons feed a good deal on buds and florets in the woods, though rape in leaf and when coming into flower is always to some extent on the menu. But the boom times are coming again with the ripening of the cereal harvest; barley first, then wheat. There's so much to choose from, and corn is so abundant, that the birds can gather the few ounces of grain they need daily in one or two hours. During this period, parent birds also take a small amount of insect food, mainly snails, woodlice and sometimes earthworms. It seems likely that with young in the nest the adults need a higher protein diet. Although I personally have cleaned many thousands of summer pigeons and examined hundreds of crop contents, I have never been aware of insect food being present, but it is highly probable that I missed the odd item because I was not expecting it.

Despite the abundance of cereal food, the birds are extremely selective about where they will dine. One particular field, and even one corner of that field, may be set upon and the rest ignored. This, if he can find that right spot in the right field, can be the high point of the pigeon shooter's year. From the end of June until the harvest is combined, birds will come to well set-out decoys. Moreover, because the majority of wood pigeons are now nesting, they will, with luck, come in ones and twos, in a steady trickle and not in a great flock. One parent bird, remember, remains at the nest incubating or looking after and feeding young. This shift system helps to ensure a steady procession rather than a mass onslaught.

Because daylight lasts now until nine or ten in the evening, birds do not have to start feeding so early, though there is often a dawn patrol of which few pigeon guns take advantage. They know that they need not be in their hides until midday, sometimes even later, and may well still be shooting at seven in the evening.

Harvest is followed by a stubbling period. The combine does not by any means pick up all the grain. The pickings are rich for pigeons feeding young. But this plenty can be short-lived. In a dry summer the farmer gets his machinery on to the land as soon as possible. In these days of high pressure farming, stubbles are ploughed up increasingly quickly. The loose grain the pigeons would otherwise have fed on well into autumn is turned in behind the tractor.

There is another kind of stubble which draws the birds like a magnet, surprisingly so in view of the tiny size of the seed found on it when compared with a grain of wheat or barley. The rape seed left behind by the combine is about the size of a radish seed and inconspicuously brown. It is obviously high in food value and fortunate is the shooter who has a well-favoured oilseed rape stubble which the farmer leaves for a week or two after his grain stubbles have been harrowed and ploughed. Birds can be lured beautifully on to a stand of decoys set up among the stiff, six-inch long stalks.

After the stubbles have disappeared, shooters are often back on lean times. In heavy acorn and beech mast years, the birds return to forage on the acorn and beech harvest in the woods, and there is little that the decoy artist can do about it.

Before the advent of oilseed rape, pigeons in winter faced very hard times indeed. The staple that kept them going was clover on leys and pastures. Clover, sometimes grown especially for fodder, including pig feed, supplemented by weed seeds, helped the wood pigeon to overwinter. In hard weather, and particularly in snow, the flocks attacked the only crops they could reach—turnip tops, kale, cabbages and Brussels sprouts. This pattern, at least, has not changed. Some of these are desperation foods. In prolonged periods of snow, the birds soon lose condition badly. Kale, particularly, seems to go right through them without producing much in the way of nourishment. But the vast acreages of winter- and spring-sown oilseed rape have dramatically changed the hard-weather menu in favour of the wood pigeon.

So much for what the wood pigeon hordes feed on. But how do they find what is best and most nourishing at any given time of the year and how do they capitalise on their discoveries?

It seems a fair guess that the delicacies they feed on courtesy of the farmer are extensions of, or closely resemble, the items they ate before the days of intensive agriculture, when the wood pigeon was a bird primarily of the forest, feeding mainly among the trees. In those far-off days, it must have found weeds to its liking in forest clearings, as it still does in meadows, leys and pastures. The farmer's clover, for example, was simply an extension of this food niche. The same goes for grain which replaced weed seeds, acorns and beech mast and was a good deal more reliable. Some years are non-cropping years in the autumn beech and oak woods. The clovers and cereals, and now oilseed rape, which mono-culture farming produces in great quantities, were ready-made for exploitation by the wood pigeon. With its capacious crop, the bird was ideally equipped to make the most of the bounty.

Pigeon shooters are apt to credit the bird with a sagacity it does not truly possess. Like all birds, the wood pigeon, cautious and wary as it certainly is, does not possess an intelligence as we know it. Though it is plainly a keen observer of its own environment, it cannot reason. It reacts to a repertoire of chemical or behavioural stimuli.

It does not, for instance, say to itself: 'They'll be sowing peas next. Let's knock off the rape and switch to peas.' When the farmer first drills his peas, they are often not discovered immediately. It is doubtful if a wood pigeon can recognise a bare field that has been drilled and rolled as a potential pea, or for that matter bean, feast though it is just possible a few experienced birds may do so. What is far more likely is that a few of the maybe thousands of pigeons in the district land on the field more or less by chance and discover peas that have not been properly rolled in—even modern farm machinery does not press them all well down into the drills, much to the pigeon's and pigeon shooter's delight and benefit. While these early birds are helping themselves, others flying over, perhaps to a rape or turnip field which they have been hammering for some weeks, see the feeding signals unwittingly transmitted by the fortunate pea-finders either on the ground or gliding in to join those already guzzling. The signal may be the nodding white neck ring of a pea-picking pigeon or the flashing white wing bars as another bird turns into the wind to land.

It does not take long for the message to get around: peas are on the menu. Soon a sizeable flock is making the most of any surface peas. Once the field is discovered, it is well within the pigeon's capability to remember exactly where the field is in relation to its home woods. Pigeons may not be very bright in a human sense but, as their racing relatives so brilliantly demonstrate, they have a great sense of direction.

Here again, Dr Murton and his field assistants did marvellous work on how the bird goes about finding the food, once it has located the field. Having landed on the chosen field, wood pigeons hunt by sight. As they move about the field they can spot anything edible up to a foot away. Murton's field-workers worked out that the average 'pace' of a feeding wood pigeon was about 4.2 inches. They then counted how many paces a bird took when feeding on a winter pasture for clover and found that the ground covered by the 'search-line' was about three-quarters of a mile daily. This meant that the pigeons had searched about one tenth of an acre each.

Perhaps more interestingly, they also discovered that the rate of food collection increased as the short winter day wore on. Until midday, the birds had very little in their crops, a phenomenon often observed by pigeon shooters who, on cleaning their bag for the freezer, exclaim in bewilderment: 'Half of them have got nothing in them!' The answer is that they stoke up late in the day so that their crop contents will last them at roost through the night. Richard Arnold explains this well in his book *Pigeon Shooting* (Faber & Faber, 1956):

A full crop has periodical contractions of its walls which force a further supply of food into the gizzard. A continuous process of receiving and passing on food is undergone by the crop during the day. Pigeons have an empty crop in the mornings, and in the winter in particular, have a full crop at evening.

Though their feed niches do overlap to some extent, each of the four pigeon and dove species in Britain has become adapted to feeding mainly on different food items. Thus, the stock dove is far better at finding small seeds, particularly weed seeds, on bare fields. In this way competition is avoided. This is a common occurrence among wild animals sharing a similar habitat. For example, zebra and many species of antelope graze the African savannas. In the main, each species prefers either a different grass or a different part of the same grass.

That yellow eye of the wood pigeon has incredible powers of focus. At long range it can spot the movement of a human face or hand. To find its food it must spot an item as small as an oilseed rape seed at a distance of a few inches. A wood pigeon can pick up fifteen grains of barley a minute in a field in which the combine has only left one grain per square foot. A man on his hands and knees in that field would be hard put to match this performance. The pigeon is helped by what the behaviourist, Niko Tinbergen, called 'a specific search image'. What this means is that the individual creature develops a mind's-eye image of what it is looking for. Once it has seen enough of this particular item, it becomes fixated on it to the exclusion of all other temptations. You can see the same thing with a feeding fish. When a hatch of a certain fly begins, the trout may at first appear to ignore it. Soon they discovered that it is good to eat, or remember the fact from previous experience, and start to take it in preference to all other insects on the water. They have adjusted their search image to the mayfly or perhaps the iron blue. For a time they will rise to nothing else. Fortunate is the angler who discovers this temporary fixation soon enough and ties the appropriate imitation fly to the end of his cast.

A wood pigeon that has adjusted its search image to a grain of barley is better equipped to find it on the stubbles than it would be if searching at random. Tests in which wheat, peas and clover were spread on a field revealed that the pigeons tuned in their search images to the food in the order they naturally preferred, namely wheat first, then peas and clover last. Birds that tried to sample all three did far worse in terms of food gathering than those who were single-minded in their selection. Tests also showed that size and shape rather than colour were the most important stimuli when it came to collecting food items.

It seems probable that such food preferences are innate, that the young are hatched with them already in place. The food given to them by parents at the nest possibly reinforces these preferences. Experience and learning in the wild does the rest. Experience may also help a few adult birds to recognise the sort of habitat that is likely to be productive of food. This might account for the first reconnaissance parties that land 'on spec' on a bare earth field and discover that it has been newly drilled with peas. If so, the birds are, as always, reacting to stimuli. In this case, the stimulus could well be the general surroundings, namely a flat recently rolled field of bare earth.

So this is how the wood pigeon hordes find and exploit the farmer's cash crops. But what damage do they actually do and how much does that damage cost the nation?

It would help, of course, if we knew exactly how many of the varmints there are. Never mind 'knowing exactly', we don't even know roughly, at least within a million or so, how many wood pigeons there are in this country.

In the 1950s and 1960s Dr Murton made an estimate of 5.8 million at the end of the breeding season. Before him, the distinguished ornithologist, James Fisher, had put the population at one and a quarter million, which was obviously far too low. He based his calculations on the field census undertaken by workers of the British Trust for Ornithology. But this census was taken in May when a fair proportion, say twenty per cent of the birds would have been nesting and would therefore not be showing themselves in full force in the open fields for counting—or anyway as near to counting as you can get with a bird as widely distributed as the wood pigeon. Murton reckoned that this May figure needed to be multiplied by five to give a figure somewhere close to the true total at the end of the summer breeding season.

Murton's sums were largely worked out on the intensively studied MAFF 2,647-acre research area at Carlton in Cambridgeshire. The wood pigeon population was accurately measured there over a six-year period. In July the average population per hundred acres was sixty-three birds increasing to 154 birds after the breeding season in September, and dropping to about seventy per hundred acres in February as a result of winter die-off. (More about this winter-kill later.)

Justifiably, Murton reckoned Carlton to be typical of intensive summer cereal cropping followed by clover and roots in winter. He then calculated what the population would be in similarly farmed areas of Britain, allowing for smaller numbers in less cultivated and wooded districts. His final estimate, he calls it an approximation, was a total British population of not less than five million birds in July rising to a probable ten million in September.

At the moment of writing, in 1994, it seems likely that, thanks to the spread of oilseed rape, wood pigeon numbers exceed that figure but, if so, no one yet knows by how much. I have, however, heard scientists hazard that at peak periods there may be as many as twenty million, though none of them would go on record as saying so. It is hoped that the BASC, Game Conservancy, BTO and MAFF researches described at the start of this book will come up with a figure we can all believe in.

For want of a more exact figure, let's work on a population of fifteen million birds. Fifteen million birds can do the farmer a considerable amount of no-good though not all the damage is as disastrous as it first appears when the flocks have finished their attack.

Clover usually recovers well, unless it is wanted for winter feed during the period in which attacks by pigeon are the most severe. Cabbages and kale can take a dreadful hammering in hard and snowy weather, simply because their leaves are accessible above the snow. Cabbages, however, often show a remarkable ability to recover, though the farmer cannot be expected to be pleased when he sees his crop shredded and torn, even though he may know that recovery is eventually likely.

Brussels sprouts are particularly vulnerable in snowy conditions. During the exceptionally hard winter of 1962-3, sprouts growers in Bedfordshire alone reckoned that pigeons cost them £250,000 then. Even so, the damage would have been much more serious if half the crop had not already been harvested before the snow fell.

A farmer friend of mine planted a twenty-acre field with young sprouts in late autumn. He was not aware at the time of an exceptional number of pigeons in the area. Two hours after first light next morning, he visited the field to find every single one of the young sprouts had had its heart picked out, presumably by pigeons. Though there was not a pigeon on the field when he arrived, he swore that there was nothing else that could have done the damage. Presumably, a large flock had moved in just after dawn and slaughtered the lot. It cost him £2,000 to replant the field. An agricultural expert, a friend of mine, suggested the real villains might have been slugs!

Wood pigeons are especially fond of peas at almost all stages of planting, growth and ripening. At one time, pea farmers in Norfolk, Huntingdonshire and the Fens had to give up pea growing altogether.

Even if some of these green crops recover, the problem is often aggravated because the modern grower may be contracted to deliver to the canner by a certain date. If wood pigeons have set back this date, then the farmer loses his money, even though the eventual crop may be a normal one. An early infestation by a large flock may mean that the farmer has to drill his field and start all over again with loss in both material and man-hours. Again, extra fertiliser is sometimes needed to help a crop such as cabbages recover.

Damage to cereal crops is not confined to eating grain. Wood pigeons will often flatten large patches of wheat or barley to get at the ears. I recall walking out along the 'tramlines' left by the sprayer to set up a hide under an oak in the middle of a wheat field and getting a bad fright when I put up fully three hundred pigeons right beside the track. They were concentrated on a patch barely ten yards square. Until the birds took off with a roar of wings, I had not even been aware they were there. There was little doubt what this mass of pigeons was doing: they were trampling and flattening an area, with the result that the wheat ears became more accessible. Almost certainly, this was not a conscious effort on their part. I can only guess that there had originally been a small laid patch of corn which a few birds flying over had spotted. They had landed and attracted others. The process of trampling had begun, and once started, had proved profitable to all concerned. The rest of the field—except a small patch around the oak tree towards which I was headed—was standing tall and upright. Quite apart from any grain lost, the trampled wheat would have taken longer to ripen and been harder to harvest efficiently.

In his *Pigeon Shooting*, first published in 1963, Archie Coats did some sums based on his own extensive experience:

A pigeon will eat up to 1,000 to 1,300 grains of wheat a day. In July or August this would be about one and a half cropfuls. A cropful weighs up to three and a half ounces. It takes thirty ounces of wheat to make a one and a half pound loaf of white bread. Therefore, a pigeon eats a loaf, or its equivalent in grain, every six days.

A pigeon [he went on with, one senses, more feeling] will eat 800 to 900 grains of malting quality barley in a day. Barley swells more than wheat, but the birds will still get through one and a half cropfuls in summer which weigh about three to four ounces. It takes three ounces of malting quality to make 1.18 pints of mild ale. Therefore, the thirsty and envious will note that a pigeon can live, like the Latuka tribesman of Equatorial Sudan, in an alcoholic stupor for most of the summer months. Foolish birds, they prefer wheat.

Perhaps more scientifically, Dr Murton recorded that a wood pigeon requires around two ounces of cereal or half a pound of fresh green food each day. Multiply that today by perhaps fifteen million and you have the size of the problem—nearly 750 tons of cereal or over 3,300 tons of fresh greens! Murton's estimate of the farmer's bill in the pre-rape days of the mid-1960s was between one and two million pounds. This was based on a probable population of five million birds. Treble that number, scale up the cost to 1994 rates and add in the bill for oilseed rape, and you have a figure more like £50 million. Perhaps we shall be nearer to the true cost when the current BASC research programme itself ripens in five years time.

The oilseed rape which has swamped much of the countryside in a yellow tide since the 1970s has proved a bonanza, and indeed a winter and early spring life-line, for the wood pigeon. The flocks attack the small green rape plants most severely in the cold months at the start of the year.

A satellite picture taken when most of the oilseed rape crop was in bloom shows the map of England as almost totally yellow. At the time the picture was taken there were said to be 1,000 square miles of this crop. Oilseed rape arrived in the 1970s. It was immediately popular as a cash crop. An added bonus was that it required little new machinery to plant or harvest. The first plantings were in Oxfordshire. From there the yellow tide spread north. It was soon into Yorkshire and then started to envelop Scotland as far as Aberdeen. But there was a snag, and the snag was the wood pigeon. The bird's depredations became so severe that by the 1980s many farmers were thinking of coming out of rape, and not a few did so. In some areas the yield was down by nine per cent, which meant the combines were picking up 2.42 tons per acre instead of 2.65. Each acre attacked by the wood pigeon flocks was costing the farmer an average of £52 in lost seed, plus additional costs for difficulties in spraying and combining. Pigeon damage meant uneven flowering so that the spraying had to be done at a time that was the least harmful for bees, which was by no means always the most economical time for the farmer. A survey revealed that losses per field varied from £306 to £1,092. Really heavy pigeon damage resulted in seeds with a far lower oil content.

EU subsidies persuaded the farmers to continue growing oilseed rape. The acreage peaked in 1991, nearly a million acres under cultivation. There are now signs that the total is beginning to fall slightly, though there is still plenty for the wood pigeon. In any case, there are compensations for the greedy bird. New 'double-low' varieties of oilseed rape are now being grown in some areas on set-aside land. (The low refers to the low level of glucosinolate.) This crop is hoped to supply industrial oil including, possibly, motor fuel. It has been found to be extremely palatable to mammals, especially hares. Who knows what the discerning gourmet pigeon will make of it? Again, linseed, a crop that gives relief to the eye with its lavender blue flowers—a nice change from brilliant yellow—is on the increase. It is said that pigeons have a taste for it in its early stages of growth, though I have no personal experience of this. A friend tells me he has had good shoots on linseed both when newly planted and in flower.

An excellent paper, *Wood Pigeons, Wood Pigeon Shooting and Agriculture*, a report to the Council of the British Association for Shooting and Conservation, compiled in 1993 by Nicola Reynolds and John Harradine, BASC research scientists, sums up the damage to the rape crop. The report, which initiated BASC's research project, quotes Dr Ian Inglis, R.K. Murton's

5

The Most Studied Bird

THE village of Carlton lies in a shallow bowl of hills a few miles from Six Mile Bottom in Cambridgeshire. The rich agricultural land in these parts is ideal wood pigeon country. It has everything a wood pigeon needs—nesting cover in the form of small, isolated woods and, until recently, a rich pattern of cereal crops. It was this combination that drew the attention of the man whose name became synonymous with the study and understanding of the bird that does so much damage to British agriculture. The man, whose name has appeared frequently in previous chapters, was Dr R.K. Murton. Indeed, twenty-six years after Murton's death, it is impossible to discuss almost any aspect of wood pigeon behaviour and biology without quoting the work of Dr Murton.

I met Ron Murton once and that was on the Medway estuary saltings in company with the late Dr Jeffery Harrison. Jeffery, fanatical wildfowler and Honorary Biologist to the then Wildfowlers Association of Great Britain and Ireland (WAGBI), now the British Association for Shooting and Conservation (BASC), had taken Murton duck flighting on Greenborough Island in the hope, I believe, that he might make him a convert, or anyway modify his attitude, to shooting. He need not have bothered. Though Ron Murton declared that he had no interest in shooting, he was neither for nor against it. Where the subject of his almost obsessive study of the wood pigeon was involved his concern was purely scientific, as to the effectiveness, or otherwise, of shooting as a way of controlling the pigeon population and thus protecting crops. A number of shooting people never came to understand this. In time, the name of Murton was to become to this small faction about as well thought of as that of Hitler or Attila the Hun. This minority never appreciated the depth and skill of his research. Speak to any scientist today working in the same general area and they instantly acknowledge his accomplishments. Scientifically speaking, Murton was, and still is, 'Dr Wood Pigeon'. For this reason, no book about the wood pigeon is complete without at least some picture of the man.

Ronald Keith Murton was born in Suffolk in May, 1932. Tony Isaacson, his long-time assistant in the field at Carlton, told me that Murton once described himself as 'being useless as a boy, but at fourteen things started to click for me'. Murton was educated at Northgate Grammar School, Ipswich, and gained a good Honours degree in Zoology at University College, London. In 1955, he got the job as an ornithologist with the Ministry of Agriculture, Fisheries and Food that was to take him immediately into the world of the wood pigeon.

In fact, within a few months it was very nearly to take him out of this world altogether. His work with the Ministry was aimed at understanding the pigeon as a threat to agriculture, the actual damage it did and, if possible, the means of avoiding or controlling that damage. The question of whether our resident population of pigeons was reinforced by large migrations from the continent had never been resolved. It was clearly a key question. So, as a step towards unravelling this mystery, the Ministry proposed that Murton be attached to the Goodwin Sands lightship for a period. Lightships and lighthouses are well-known magnets to migrating birds of many species. It was hoped that from this seaborne vantage point Murton would be able to observe the existence or absence of cross-Channel pigeon movements.

He hadn't been long on board when the bottom started to fall out of the barometer. It became plain that a serious storm was on the way. The crew thought nothing of such tempests. A lightship, they said, could weather anything. As the wind increased to storm force, Murton poked his head out on deck and noticed that the coastline was moving. The ship was meant to be unbreakably anchored to the sea bed. When he suggested to the crew that they were adrift, no one took the landlubber seriously. Stay below, beneath battened hatches they said, and all would be well. When Murton saw water sluicing about below decks, he decided that he would have no chance if the ship foundered. Up on deck the wind force was appalling. His analytical mind told him that the best place to be if the ship went aground would be lashed to the lamphouse. That was where the lifeboat crew found him when the storm finally blew itself out. He had a vague recollection of some poor fellow clinging to his legs before he was swept away. Murton was the only survivor. As a result of exposure to salt water, he was 'sea-blind' for several days afterwards. He resolved henceforward to do all his work ashore. He recorded the experience with typical scientific detachment in a paper on migration published by himself and his co-worker M.G. Ridpath in 1961:

> Observations from the South Goodwin light vessel by one of us (R.K.M.) from 1 November until she was wrecked on 27 November showed that no wood pigeon flights could be seen at sea four miles due east of St Margaret's Bay.

Murton was not the first ornithologist to approach the problem of the wood pigeon's agricultural depredations. The Second World War with its need to grow food on every available acre had focussed attention on the pigeon's unconscious alliance with the U-Boat. A distinguished scientist, M.K. Colquhoun, was commissioned by the Agricultural Research Council to head a team to study the wood pigeon. The team was to work in collaboration with the British Trust for Ornithology (BTO) with support in the field from many of its amateur bird-watchers. Colquhoun was given research facilities at the Edward Grey Institute of Field Ornithology at Oxford. His brief was to approach the wood pigeon as entirely harmful to the nation and the emphasis was to be on control. In his monograph, *The Wood Pigeon*, Murton is full of praise for his predecessor:

> Although Colquhoun's approach was essentially that of the biologist, his research was done under economic pressure and at a time when modern ideas of bird or other animal ecology were hardly formulated. It is to the credit

of Colquhoun and his staff that the methods they adopted and the results they produced to a large extent pioneered the post-war upsurge in bird ecology.

Colquhoun's report, published in 1951, reached a conclusion which makes strange reading today.

> There is enough evidence to state confidently that there is no need to take special steps to control the wood pigeon population in the near future. This is due to two wartime factors, the decreased shooting of predatory birds and the increased shooting of wood pigeons, as a result of which it seems likely that the wood pigeon population will decline to a lower level than had been known in living memory .... It would be wise to await the full effect of the aftermath of the war from which the wood pigeon as well as man is still suffering.

For several years, nothing much was done about the wood pigeon problem. Then, in the early 1950s, pressure from the farming community led the Ministry of Agriculture to begin a full-time research programme. This was where Ron Murton came on the scene.

Born and brought up in East Anglia, it was natural that Murton should look to his own part of England for a study area. He had no doubt about the size of the pigeon population. Andrew Wylie, Cambridgeshire Pest Officer, suggested that he visit Carlton. Wylie had excellent relationships with the landowners there (now the Vestey family) and even offered Murton a 'home from home' in the middle of his study area.

Topographically, the study area at Carlton has changed little though it has been added to since the early 1960s by the cultivation of an old wartime airstrip. (By the end of the century, it may have changed out of all recognition. There are plans to flood the valley to form a new reservoir.) In the early days of Murton's study, spring barley was the main crop, with winter wheat running second. Ten per cent of the total 2,647 acres) was permanent pasture with good supplies of clover to tide the pigeons through the winter. Recently, the cropping has altered considerably. There is much grass and no oilseed rape, with the result that by 1994, when I visited it, the pigeon population had fallen dramatically. In common with much intensively-cultivated farmland, many small hedgerows have been grubbed out since Murton's study began in the late 1950s. Five woods and large hawthorn hedges, however, provide the pigeons with over eighty acres of fine nesting cover. From the point of view of Murton and his team of observers, Carlton had one other thing to recommend it. Its undulating countryside provides excellent vantage points from which to observe pigeons in pastures, feeding on crops, as well as on flight lines in and out of the woods.

Andrew Wylie's introduction quickly secured Murton the co-operation of farmers and keepers. By 1955, the Carlton project had been set up. As invaluable colleagues in the field Murton had Tony Isaacson and N.J. Westwood, without whom much of the fantastically thorough programme of the next twelve years would have been impossible.

Murton's approach was that no conclusions could be reached about wood pigeon numbers, the actual damage they did, the cost of that damage to farming and, eventually, possible methods of effective control until far more basic information about the bird had been obtained. So he and his fellow workers set out to unravel the hitherto unknown, or anyway uncertain, details of wood pigeon ecology and behaviour. 'Proper diagnosis,' he wrote, 'usually precedes any remedy and although the empirical approach sometimes produces an answer it is not the best method to adopt when the problem is complicated.' In the next twelve years, often jointly with his co-workers Tony Isaacson and N.J. Westwood, he published more than fifty papers on the wood pigeon and related problems. The 2,000 odd acres at Carlton became probably the most scientifically studied area of farmland in Britain and the wood pigeon Britain's most investigated bird. In 1962 London University awarded him a PhD for his pigeon studies.

It would be tedious and probably impossible in this book to give a full account of the methods used by Murton and his team in the field but a brief description of some of these will be of interest. His conclusions are what really count in the saga of the wood pigeon. These conclusions, as we shall see, caused a considerable furore in the shooting world.

To obtain the vital information about wood pigeon biology, nest surveys, later carried out by his successor, Dr Ian Inglis, were conducted every two weeks. Murton held that weekly inspections might cause too much nest disturbance and therefore give an advantage to predators. A set route was followed through the nesting areas. As each nest was found it was marked with a numbered metal tag, special care being taken to look for any nests started since the previous visit.

Nest searching became more difficult once the trees were in full leaf. A check was made at the end of the breeding season when the leaves had been shed in order to spot any nests (now deserted of course) that had been missed earlier. The number of nests monitored by Ian Inglis between 1962 and 1983 (the figures then would have been much the same in Murton's time) varied between sixteen and 122 with an average of forty-five per season.

The interior of the nest was examined by means of a mirror attached to a telescopic pole. A record card for each nest showed when the eggs were laid and when they hatched, when the young were fledged, and the number and fate of each egg and juvenile. From such a programme it was possible to estimate very accurately the breeding success of the Carlton population of some 3,000 birds.

Observation of feeding flocks, winter and summer, gave a clear picture of food preferences, feeding rates, methods of feeding, weight gained or lost as the result of feeding on different crops, the amount of various crops taken in a given time by individual birds, yearly variations in pigeon densities as well as in breeding success and even the probable cost per pigeon per year to the British farmer.

Most of the work was done on foot and with notebook in hand, though hi-tech aids were sometimes used. By means of fitting a small radio transmitter to a young pigeon taken from the nest when nearly fully fledged, Tony Isaacson, for example, was able to follow that individual bird's movements throughout the day. The technique, known as telemetry, is now widely used on everything from tigers to hedgehogs. A strong-flying bird like a wood pigeon, apparently, does not feel at all inconvenienced by wearing a miniature waistcoat and trailing a light radio antenna. The minute transmitter emits a signal detectable at ranges of up to three miles. Isaacson was therefore able to observe not only his subject's movements but to monitor its feeding behaviour. Having pinpointed it, he could observe through binoculars how many pecks it took at, say, clover, for how long, the distance between pecks and the total area covered in a food search. At one stage it was decided to try rocket-netting pigeons decoyed to an area pre-baited with tic beans in order to obtain more birds for telemetry and ringing. Unlike wildfowl, including geese, which are regularly caught by this method, the pigeons were too quick off the mark for the net. By the time its folds should have enveloped them they had escaped at the sides and flown away.

Perhaps the best way to give some picture of the size and scope of Murton's work is to list some of the papers he published between 1958 and 1964. Here is a selection: *The Breeding of Wood Pigeon Populations*, 1958; *Visible Migration in N.E. Norfolk in November*, 1956; *The Effect on Wood Pigeon Breeding of Systematic Nest Destruction*, 1960; *Some Photographs of Wood Pigeon Behaviour and Feeding*, 1960 [Murton was an excellent photographer]; *Some Survival Estimates for the Wood Pigeon*, 1961; *The Ecology of Wood Pigeon Populations with Special Reference to Their Breeding Biology*, Murton and Isaacson, *A Functional Basis of Some Behaviour in the Wood Pigeon*, 1962; *Productivity and Egg Predation in the Wood Pigeon*; *The Autumn Movements of Wood Pigeon*, 1962; Murton and Vizoso, *Dressed Cereal Seed as a hazard to Wood Pigeons*, 1963; Murton and Westwood, *The Food Preferences of Pheasants and Wood Pigeons in Relation to the Selective use of Stupefying baits*; Murton, Isaacson and Westwood, *The Feeding Ecology of the Wood Pigeon*, 1963; *The Food and Growth of Nestling Wood Pigeons in Relation to the Breeding Season*, 1963; *The Use of Baits Treated with Alphachlorolose to Catch Wood Pigeons*, 1963; Murton, Westwood and Isaacson, *The Feeding Habits of the Wood Pigeon, Stock Dove and Turtle Dove*, 1964; *A Preliminary Investigation of the Factors Regulating Population Size in the Wood Pigeon* . . . to name, as they say, but a few.

It is with the last paper that we reach Ron Murton's most contentious finding—that winter-kill through food shortage, NOT shooting, controlled the wood pigeon population. This, taken with the experimental use of the stupefying chemical alphachorolose gave a new meaning to that ancient cliché 'cat among the pigeons'. As far as the shooting community was concerned there was no doubt who was the cat.

Murton's finding that shooting was an ineffectual and costly means of controlling the wood pigeon was bad enough. There is no doubt that feathers were further ruffled by several of the Doctor's recorded opinions on wood pigeon shooting, for example: 'I derive no satisfaction from shooting—other than with a camera—and for me it only serves as a means to an end; consequently I cannot discourse on the merits of pigeon shooting as a sport.' . . . . and: 'Surely we should woo the day when the need arises to introduce a close season to protect the wood pigeon from the ravages of the hunger.'

It goes without saying that any man is entitled to express his views on the ethics of shooting, even of a public enemy. It was, however, the weight of scientific evidence that Murton brought to bear that really caused the 'pigeons', or rather dedicated pigeon shooters, to fly up in panic.

To get the full picture, it is necessary briefly to recap the history of the Ministry of Agriculture's brief love affair, or anyway liaison, with the pigeon shooter. In 1953, largely as a result of M.K. Colquhoun's investigation into the depredations caused by the wood pigeon (*The Wood Pigeon in Britain*, 1951), the Ministry introduced a cartridge subsidy scheme. Half-price cartridges were issued to pigeon shooters recognised by the County Pest Officers as competent and genuine. All that was needed to get this bonus was a receipt for cartridges and a record of the number of pigeons shot. Secretaries of recognised pigeon clubs could obtain cartridges in the same way and distribute them to their members. Some of the cartridges were used by decoy shooters but most were blown off in grand battues, or roost shoots, that took place in the woods, mainly in February and March after the game shooting season had ended.

In 1965, the subsidy was withdrawn, amid a good deal of opposition from the shooting community, largely as the result of research at Carlton which had shown that the battues did nothing to reduce the pigeon population. However, the subsidy did not entirely or immediately disappear. Rabbit Clearance Societies had originally been introduced by the Ministry to keep control of rabbits. By the 1960s, myxomatosis had vastly reduced the rabbit population, and the farmers were demanding that more action be taken against that other menace, the wood pigeon. Since the mechanism of the Rabbit Clearance Societies still remained, it was convenient to be able to issue farmers and accredited pigeon guns with half-price cartridges for pigeon control through the RCS network. In 1969, because of a change in government policy towards financial support for farming, the Societies were abolished and half-price cartridges disappeared. Against this background, any further moves interpreted as anti-pigeon shooting were bound to be viewed with disapproval by the shooting community.

Murton's years of research at Carlton had, he claimed, proved beyond doubt that shooting did not materially affect, let alone control, pigeon numbers. The result of shooting in the Carlton area, he argued, was to kill birds that would in any case die of other causes, notably starvation in winter. While he conceded that the conclusions his team had reached were the result of painstaking research on some 2,647 acres of Cambridgeshire, there was every reason to suppose that they were typical of other heavily farmed pigeon-rich areas.

In general, though shooting pressure had been heavy throughout Britain for many years, he stated, there was no evidence of a decline of pigeon numbers at a national level. To bring about the latter, it would be necessary to kill more birds in a year than could be replaced by reproduction—then estimated at 2.4 surviving young per pair. To achieve this, shooting pressure would have to be more than doubled. He illustrated his argument in the following way.

If all the birds shot at Carlton during February and March— twenty pigeons per hundred acres on average—could have been shot in December, the population in December would have been reduced by about twenty per cent. If no shooting at all took place in December, yearly counts had shown that the population by the end of February would still be very much the same, in other words reduced by around twenty per cent. What would have killed them? Murton's answer was shortage of winter food. In other words, winter-kill was the factor that controlled pigeon numbers, not shooting. His argument was scientifically unassailable, though that did not prevent a good many shooters from trying to demolish it.

Foremost amongst these was David Lishman, a chartered patent agent from Solihull, in Warwickshire. Lishman was a member of WAGBI's management committee and Hon. Secretary of the Midlands Wood Pigeon Club, motto: 'Pigeon shooters at your service'. The club had thirty members, all decoy experts, who shot free of charge to farmers to protect their crops. They had access for this purpose to over 30,000 acres. David Lishman was, therefore, an intensely interested party when it came to contesting Murton's conclusions. He attacked on many fronts, always in a rational and reasonable way but there was little doubt that he was, understandably, emotionally and intellectually biased in his arguments intended to support the case for control by shooting.

Lishman wrote many articles in the sporting press and enlisted the aid of prominent figures in field sports including the professional, Archie Coats, of whom more later. Lishman provoked considerable controversy, even inside WAGBI itself, when reviewing Murton's papers and monograph for various WAGBI publications. Between 1967 and 1969 he initiated his own investigations into wood pigeon biology as well as into the attitude of the shooting community towards Murton's findings. The main area in which Lishman challenged Murton was his contention that shooting failed as a control mechanism on wood pigeons. Lishman argued that shooting at Carlton had simply been of the battue or roost shooting type, in which Lishman himself had little faith. Murton had not taken into proper account the effectivenes of decoy shooting to protect a vulnerable crop.

Lishman challenged Murton's statement that 'the wood pigeon is not a bird of *la chasse* as it is in France'. His survey of WAGBI affiliated clubs included the question: 'Do your members regard the wood pigeon as an important sporting bird?' Ninety-nine per cent of the seventy-nine clubs responding gave a resounding 'yes'.

In a paper published in 1964, Murton had maintained that some thirty-six per cent of post-breeding wood pigeon populations died between September and December, eighteen per cent between December and February and five per cent between February and July.

In a series of papers of his own, Lishman rejected the Murton team's hypothesis that winter wood pigeon populations were regulated by their winter food supply, or lack of it, the staple of this food source being clover. Lishman's answer to this was to the effect: 'In that case, why doesn't one see pigeon corpses littering the countryside?' To counter the claim that vast numbers died of winter starvation, Lishman instigated, through WAGBI clubs, a survey of the body-weights of pigeons shot in the winter months in an attempt to prove that the birds weren't losing condition due to food shortage. For several years the Lishman–Murton controversy—the controversy was all on Lishman's side—created an interesting stir in the sporting press. At the end of it all, nothing much was changed. No cartridge subsidy had been lost because none then existed. Wood pigeons went their own historic and destructive way. Shooting continued, in fact, undoubtedly increased as more and more 'lone wolf' shooters, as Murton called them, discovered, learned and became fascinated by the art of decoying. Murton's work remained unscathed by it all, though many of the factors affecting the bird itself were to change in the next two decades rendering some of his findings out of date.

I have come across one fascinating document from the era of what might be called 'the great wood pigeon controversy'. It is a reply from the Regional Pest Officer for Staffordshire to questions put by Lishman to Ron Murton in June 1965. An extract reads:

I confirm that wood pigeons have for many years been the target of an intensive shooting campaign and certainly no other pest species has been a greater target though, even so, the effort has been futile. [Lishman contended that there had never been a concentrated and organised campaign against the bird. The reply continues.] Dr Murton claims that the amount of shooting could not be increased sufficiently at an economical cost to make any difference. If shooting was of any use, it would have stopped the populations recovering from a two-thirds reduction after the hard winter of 1962-3 in only two years. You may argue that you reduced your efforts when the population was low but one of our contentions is that when a population falls to a low level hunting pressure falls.

Somehow, I detect in this answer a degree of tetchiness that suggests the Ministry, and Dr Murton, were getting a bit fed up with the whole controversy, but that courtesy demanded a reply. David Lishman tells me that, thirty-five years later, his views on Dr Murton's researches have not substantially changed.

David Lishman was, however, not quite correct when he claimed that all the shooting at Carlton had been of the largely ineffectual—totally ineffectual in terms of population control—battue or roost shooting variety. In fact, Murton and his co-workers had fired every shot in the pigeon gun's locker. What is not well known is that they had scientifically examined and analysed the effect of decoy shooting.

The details of that experiment make intriguing reading, especially for the many 'lone wolf' specialists now enjoying the sport of pigeon decoying, and, as they would claim, protecting crops in the process. For the shooter there may be something to learn from those experiments, though the Gun who sits in a hide decoying over a field of highly vulnerable spring rape may not agree with the conclusions of Murton, Westwood and Isaacson in their 1974 paper: *A Study of Wood Pigeon Shooting: The Exploitation of a Natural Animal Population.*

In November 1967, experimental decoy shooting was started as part of the Carlton research programme. It was to last until December 1970. The Gun chosen for the job was Bill Edgar, one of the Ministry of Agriculture's Regional Pest Staff. He is described as 'an ardent and highly competent pigeon shooter'. 'It is pertinent to record,' the report adds, 'that Mr Edgar rates as a top-class decoy gunner.'

One can't help envying Bill Edgar his job. He was supplied with everything he needed, including cartridges. For the first twelve months, he shot under the scientists' direction and close observation. Every move he and the pigeons made, every bird he killed or missed, every pigeon that flew within range of the decoys and reacted to them or ignored them was noted, usually by Tony Isaacson stationed in a vehicle within sight but out of disturbance range of the decoy set-up.

During this first twelve months, Bill Edgar shot from every conceivable type of hide known to a pigeon man. No doubt, he built these himself most skilfully and with pure fieldcraft rather than by slide-rule and tape measure. It is not recorded, however, what he thought of setting out his decoys on a 'standard equal-sided grid at one metre centres'. Most decoyists lay out their decoy 'picture' using a mixture of instinct, experience and inspired guesswork. They are not, however, taking part in a scientific experiment. They are merely shooting pigeons. All credit to Bill Edgar that he did that, too, and with a cartridge average that certainly put him in the 'first eleven'. All this, mark you, when being observed through binoculars. Most of us do not shoot too well, especially from a pigeon hide, when being watched!

The number and type of decoys was constantly altered during the first year, and results observed. From five to two hundred decoys were used in various trials, sometimes dummies, sometimes dead birds, occasionally a mixture of both. The dead birds were preserved by injecting them with formalin (a device sometimes used by the keen and regular pigeon shooter). Some were dried with wings neatly folded as when feeding or at rest. Others were 'mummified' with their wings spread.

I quote from the research document: 'All wood pigeons flying over, alone or in flocks, which passed within sighting range of the decoys were noted. The number which responded by dipping towards the decoys and/or attempting to settle, the number shot at and the number killed were recorded. Records were kept of man-hour and cartridge expenditure.'

After the first year, Bill Edgar was, so to speak, let off the scientific leash. He was provided with all the cartridges he needed and given the freedom of the study area with the brief of eradicating the local wood pigeon population to the best of his considerable ability. 'Because this was an official study, Mr Edgar shot pigeons as often and whenever he considered it worthwhile,' the report goes on.

The observations concerning the numbers and types of decoys used in these experiments are of considerable interest to all serious pigeon shooters, though many of the conclusions reached will already be known or will seem fairly obvious to experienced decoy gunners:

1. Single birds were more susceptible to decoys than flocks, and small flocks more decoyable than large ones.
2. Increasing the number of decoys can increase the response of large flocks but there are limitations to the number used. Very large decoy stands may even repel birds.
3. Increase of the number of decoys from five to twenty-five resulted in an increase of response by passing single birds. There were indications that individual pigeons were more attracted to medium numbers of decoys.
4. Pigeons (if not shot at) would land next to decoys with closed wings, whereas if there were many open-winged decoys in use, birds that looked like incomers would shy away and refuse to settle.
5. Not surprisingly, artificial decoys produced a poorer response than dead birds. Comparing fifteen dead pigeons and fifteen artificials shows that the plastics resulted in thirteen per cent fewer pigeons being shot and forty-six per cent fewer when forty artificial decoys were used.
6. An increase in the number of dead pigeons with closed wings, to about eighty, or with open wings to about forty, led to an increase in the percentage response from live birds and hence numbers shot. When more than eighty decoys were put out, pigeons were repelled.

Mr Edgar must have had a wonderful time during those three years, and there is little doubt that he shot extremely well. Few could have done better. In his best month he averaged 1.4 cartridges per bird and in his worst 2.1. The conclusions were not, however, in favour of shooting as a cost-efficient method of pigeon control.

The cost in terms of man-hours and cartridges worked out at 24 pence (at 1968-9 prices), whereas, the report went on, it cost 13 pence to kill a pigeon with stupefying baits. With the latter, the man-hours per bird worked out at 0.10. The man-hours put in by Mr Edgar to achieve the same result were 0.23. The summary concluded: 'For shooting to affect population size, a cost of about 50 pence per bird would probably be realistic assuming sufficient guns were available.'

However, the paper did make one concession, or anyway part-concession, to the shooting interests:

Shooting for crop protection can only be justified in those circumstances where pigeons are prevented from attacking a vulnerable crop, and to a large extent the crop protection value of shooting depends on its acting as a scaring mechanism. It seems likely that more efficient and less costly scaring mechanisms are available. Paradoxically, because battue shooting reduced winter competition and allowed more birds to survive until spring, it probably increased the risks of crop damage once the winter season of limiting resources was passed.

There was another area in which shooting interests and the scientists met head-on—the use of stupefying baits to control pigeons. Mention was made earlier of alphachlorolose. Grain treated with chemical repellants had been tried on pigeons without success. The ideal chemical would be one that made the birds unconscious without killing them. Commercially valuable, aesthetically pleasing, protected birds or game birds could then, theoretically, be released, while the 'nasties' such as crows, jays, magpies and, of course, wood pigeon could be knocked on the head.

M.K. Colquhoun had carried out experiments between 1942 and 1945 using a substance called tribromoethanol. He caught 1,488 birds, of which sixty-one per cent were wood pigeons, thirty-six per cent corvids, two per cent protected species and one per cent gamebirds. However, the chemical, used on imitation peas made from gelatin capsules, proved too volatile when exposed to heat and sunlight. Its effects often wore off before the birds ate the 'peas'.

Alphachlorolose ($C_8H_{11}Cl_3O_6$) in fine white powder form, seemed the perfect answer. It had already been used with some success by the French. Early experiments in Britain failed because the baited area was not large enough. Trials at Carlton over a long period proved that it could be extremely effective if administered properly. The proportion of chemical to oil-coated grain was three per cent by weight. All told, 3,300 pigeons were captured by this method, some of which were ringed or fitted with radios for telemetry and released.

Some of the problems of chemical baiting could be got round, for instance the risk of killing songbirds. To avoid this all you had to do was to use a bait too big for small birds to swallow.

As could have been predicted, the shooting world became extremely concerned about the possibility of the successful and general use of alphachlorolose. What would be the rationale of shooting wood pigeons to protect crops if the farmer could more easily and cheaply prevent damage by doping them? And anyway, if chemical protection became the norm, would there be enough pigeons left to shoot?

In 1965, when Murton published his monograph *The Wood Pigeon*, the issue was still very much alive. But it became clear that conservation interests, let alone shooting ones, viewed chemical control with aversion. Moreover, there was considerable likelihood that farmers would not apply the chemical or the baited food (tic beans for preference) correctly and would in time become careless. To their credit, and despite the hideous record of organo-phosphorous seed dressings such as aldrin and dieldrin which had had a disastrous effect on wildlife, especially birds of prey, farmers disliked the idea of chemically killing birds.

Murton himself recognised this when he wrote:

Methods using stupefying baits are potentially a valuable means of control but further field tests are necessary. In theory, the object of using a narcotic is that protected game species are allowed to recover or be released unharmed. In practice, this is not entirely feasible. Any form of wood pigeon control must take into account the interests of wildlife preservation, of sporting traditions and of food production. Hence, the wood pigeon problem is a particularly difficult one.

To everyone's relief, the use of alphacholorose was abandoned. For environmental reasons, it is not likely that chemical warfare will be waged on the wood pigeon in the future.

There is a sad ending to Ron Murton's life and distinguished career. Granted a year's sabbatical in 1968, he went to work in the University of Hong Kong where he became completely absorbed in laboratory work and never returned to the field which had earned him such an international reputation. His work became so abstruse—it was concerned with the circadian (the daily recurring) rhythms of birds—that very few ornithologists could understand the scientific language used. This, apparently, belonged to the world of the endocrinologist and photobiologist. After Hong Kong he worked for the Nature Conservancy, Monks Wood Experimental Station and the Natural Environment Research Council. The University of Hull made him a professor. Ron Murton was, his former colleagues say, a good boss, exacting but a fair and always stimulating one. Above all, he was a workaholic, and this undoubtedly aggravated his heart condition. He suffered a heart attack and insisted on returning to work when his doctors advised a long rest. He died on the day he had decided to go back to his desk.

6

Pigeon Shooting,
a very short History

AMONG other pronouncements on shooting, Murton wrote:

> To a large extent shooting wood pigeons is regarded as a plebeian sport, and while it is of course unfair to generalise all rural attitudes so strongly, nevertheless it remains a fact that the wood pigeon is not a bird of *la chasse* as it is in France, and there is nothing to be gained by disguising this situation with euphemisms.

Those words were written in the 1960s. Thirty-five years later, I doubt whether many of the 300,000 or so Britons who shoot wood pigeons would agree with any of them. Many regard the bird as the prime quarry of *la chasse*. Class structures have altered inside shooting as everywhere else. Not many pigeon shooters would think of themselves as 'plebeian'. (OED definition: 'of low birth, of the common people, uncultured, coarse, base, ignoble.') It was a curiously snobby word for a grammar school boy like Ron Murton to use. Nevertheless, though he was a shade behind the times, Murton's judgement would have been fairly accurate at least until the onset of the Second World War. Nobody much shot wood pigeons from 1939–45. There were other more hostile targets to be engaged by the rural community. But, when peace came, the picture was to change dramatically. Murton's generalisation about the plebeian nature of pigeon shooters would soon be out of date. Pigeon shooting was to become a popular branch of shooting sport with a considerable spin-off benefit to agriculture.

Largely because of these earlier attitudes, it is now extremely difficult to trace the history of pigeon shooting.

Colonel Hawker, as we have seen, living in the mid-nineteenth century, in what is today prime wood pigeon country in Hampshire, only bagged one or two birds a year. But not far away, in Selborne in another part of Hampshire, Gilbert White recorded some half century earlier:

> They [wood pigeons] were shot not only as they were feeding in the fields, and especially in snowy weather, but also at the close of evening, by men who lay in ambush among the woods and groves to kill them as they came to roost.

White was born in 1720 and died in 1793. He therefore lived in the day of the flintlock muzzle-loader, a time when 'shooting flying' was only just evolving and probably not often practised among the rural community. Far more likely that they shot sitting wood pigeons on the turnips and cabbages in snow and blasted them out of the trees or as they pitched into the branches at roosting time.

However, in *The Natural History of Selborne*, his classic work of natural observation, White recorded:

> I have consulted a sportsman, now in his seventy-eighth year, who tells me that fifty or sixty years back, when the beechen woods were much more extensive than at present, the number of wood pigeons was astonishing; that he has often killed near twenty in a day; and that with a long wildfowl piece he has shot seven or eight at a time on the wing as they came wheeling over his head: he moreover adds, which I was not aware of, that often there were among them little parties of small blue doves, which he calls *rockiers*. The food of these numberless emigrants was beech mast and some acorns; and particularly barley which they collected in the stubbles. But of late years, since the vast increase of turnips, that vegetable has furnished a great part of their support in hard weather; and the holes they peck in these roots greatly damage the crop. From this food their flesh has contracted a rancidness which occasions them to be rejected by the nicer judges of eating, who thought them before a delicate dish.

White's 'rockiers', presumably named thus after the rock dove, were almost certainly stock doves. His observation about pecking at the turnips accords with modern experience. In hard weather, pigeons feed avidly on the turnip tops.

John Mills writing in a book on British sporting birds published in Edinburgh in 1845 confirms that roost shooting was the most favoured method. He also backs Gilbert White on the inedibility of turnip-eating birds!

> The wood pigeon or ring dove is the largest species of dove in England and is too well known to need a particular description. The best plan I have found, for getting within range of this watchful bird, is to take your station close to the trunk of a tree in the covert they frequent and then under this to shelter and wait for their coming. It is strange that wary as these birds are, they will perch on the branches within easy range of you without seeing the danger, if your movement be quiet and yet to steal upon them is next to impossible. Except when feeding on turnips they are very good eating.

Towards the end of the eighteenth century, someone certainly *was* shooting wood pigeons in a fairly big way. The naturalist Selby recorded:

> As some sort of recompense for the great damage it does to crops, it must be remembered that the flesh of this bird is very palatable and enormous numbers find their way into the markets.

I would love to know how those 'enormous numbers' were being harvested, presumably by market gunners. But were they shooting over decoys and how much did they know of or practise that art? I would hazard very little.

Decoys, usually for wildfowl, are known to have been in use by native people for at least two thousand years. But in Britain and for pigeon? One or two rustics may have carved their own decoys out of ash or beech but wooden decoys don't bear carrying very far. There were, of course, always dead birds to set up as decoys once you had shot the first half dozen. My guess is that the locals who Selby declares sent numbers of birds to market were mainly roost shooters.

Towards the end of the nineteenth century, well-to-do Guns were totally pre-occupied with large bags of probably not very well shown pheasants. The weekend shooting party with its romantic intrigues, snobberies and rivalries was then much in vogue. Some of this was decidedly parvenu in character and found its parallel nearly one hundred years later in the corporate shoots of the booming 1980s when the quantities of pheasants killed, not the quality of pheasants shown was the main criterion.

In those Victorian and Edwardian days, there were, of course, some classic shots, great shotgun artists and sportsmen. Just as men like John Millais, Sir Ralph Payne-Galwey and Abel Chapman 'discovered' wildfowling and punt-gunning—until then the plebeian sports carried on by longshoremen and market gunners—so did the famous game shots discover pigeon decoying and include it in the great shooting books of the period.

Lord Walsingham, one of the finest game shots of all time, gave the wood pigeon full credit as a bird of *la chasse* in the *Field and Covert* volume of the Badminton Library published in 1889. He dealt with the technique of decoying in considerable detail:

> The pigeon shooter should provide himself with three or four stuffed wood pigeons prepared for the purpose with copper wire, coming from within the body of the bird and passing down the legs, leaving about fifteen or sixteen inches projecting through each foot. He should select a convenient tree on the spot most frequented by the birds, where an active lad can climb high among the branches and fasten the decoys by means of copper wire to suitable twigs and branches, always placing their heads to the wind . . . .
>
> In snow, which is most favourable if not deep enough to prevent birds from feeding, a nightshirt put on over the shooting coat and a white flannel cap effect the purpose of concealment admirably . . . .

A high wind is almost absolutely essential for this sport. It prevents the gun from being heard at a distance, clears away the smoke, hanging among the trees on a still day, alarms the birds and not only makes them fly lower than on calm days but prevents them from seeing so well when flying against it. In such weather they will frequently settle among the decoys or on trees within shot of the sportsman.

It will be found useful to be prepared beforehand with several short sticks pointed at both ends and when ten or twelve birds are down to gather them quickly and set them up on open spaces beneath the trees as assistant decoys. With wings closed to their sides, resting on their breast bones, they can be fixed with heads erect or craning forward as if in search for food.

Walsingham thanked a Mr J.E. Harting for

the illustration of an excellent method of mounting dead wood pigeons as decoys. By cutting a number of pieces of wire netting in the shape indicated, the fresh-killed birds can be at once set up with wings clasped to their sides and heads erect either on short sticks in the ground or on the branches of trees. By means of jointed rods they can be elevated to any reasonable height without the necessity of climbing.

The wire-netting technique is one I have myself used to simulate birds with wings outstretched as if landing. The jointed rods will be recognised by anyone who uses 'lofters'.

The betting is that very few of the gentry followed the noble lord's advice, considering wood pigeons as something merely to be potted at on a driven pheasant day. One or two well-to-do shots, sportsmen who today would be called 'real shooting men', realised the bird's worth. Among them was a Mr H.F. Lawford who would have found much in common with today's experts.

I came across Mr Lawford's advice on pigeon shooting in what must be a very rare book. It is called *The House on Sport* and was published by Gale and Polden in 1898. The 'House' of the title is the London Stock Exchange. The book consists of a collection of articles on everything from archery to yachting by members of the 'House'. The proceeds from this remarkable work (which includes a unique wildfowling chapter concerning a steam driven gunning punt called 'the Ironside') went to the Children's Dinners Fund organised by *The Referee* newspaper.

Mr Lawford recounts how he took a lease of a 7,000-acre sporting estate in Scotland at the centre of which were several hundred acres of woods described by the agent as 'worthless' but which were, nonetheless, full of pigeons:

> One day, while having a tramp for partridges towards the end of September, I came to a wall bounding a barley stubble of about twenty acres and saw a blue cloud of pigeons rise off the ground and stooks: there were plenty of oat stubbles round, studded with stooks, but no birds in them.
>
> I had not long to wait for a windy day and after breakfast drove off for the field, armed with a dead pigeon, a fir bough or two and some soft wire. The fact of there not being a single pigeon in the field did not disappoint me, nor were there any to be seen in the sky, for I knew they had had breakfast at daybreak and had gone to digest it in the woods a mile or more away.
>
> With my back to a rock, a whin bush in front and a fir bough on either side, a few minutes saw a nice hide ready for a seated gunner and, with the help of the wire, I soon had my pigeon looking life-like enough perched on a stook about twenty-five yards from the hide with his head upwind.
>
> Still being no birds about, seated in my hide, I pulled out the newspaper and read it nearly through, when the noise of wings past my head made me drop the paper, seize the gun and, with a flukey shot, bring down the pigeon. Picking him up, wiring him and placing him on the ground this time, was the work of a moment but my watch told me I had been forty minutes shooting one bird. However, now I began to see black specks in the air in the distance, all coming from the same direction—the big woods—and then I knew we should be busy ere long. Each bird I shot, I ran out and wired until I had a little flock of half a dozen, some on stooks, some on the ground. After that I did not trouble to pick up any more unless they lay

on their backs too near the decoys. Towards the middle of the morning pigeons came fast enough to keep me amused .... I fired as I sat: to rise would have put them out of shot before I could fire.

When birds alight in the field where the shooting is going on, the gunner must make a noise to put them off and, if necessary, even show himself. If allowed to remain, they will act as counter decoys to his and so interfere with his sport.

After three hours and half I reckoned I had dropped sixty pigeons. The autumn I am speaking of showed a bag of close on eight hundred pigeons. It might have been far more had I been able to devote more time to them ....

Everything about this account shows that Mr Lawford knew as much about the game as most modern shooters. He knew his shoot would come good from previous reconnaissance. He set up his decoys correctly. He understood the importance of a hide that melted into the landscape. He shot *sitting*. He knew that once the birds were fixated on his decoys he need not bother to tidy up the decoy pattern too much. (This might not be the case with today's 'decoy-smart' pigeon.) He knew full well about the counter-attraction of birds settling elsewhere on his chosen field and the absolute necessity of scaring them off. That great professional Archie Coats would have touched his battered hat to him.

Despite the obviously growing interest in the sport, very little was written for the specialist pigeon shooter. However, in 1934, *Shooting Times and British Sportsman*, as the magazine was then styled, published a small book, *Sport with Wood Pigeons*, by one of its contributors, Max Baker. In his preface. Mr Baker says:

In preparing these notes I have written at length on a subject which is usually dismissed in a chapter or other brief form, with the result that much gets left out that might assist the student.

The opinions which I have submitted are not intended as laying down the law, rather as indicating the points that have to be considered in order to gain success in this fascinating branch of the sport. If any reader has cause to differ fundamentally I should be glad to hear from him. To all I would preach charity. Those who know are seldom able to write. Those who write are lucky if they can find time to know.

Max Baker certainly knew and even more certainly could write. Though later research showed his views on migration of wood pigeons from the Continent to be unsound—almost everybody got that wrong and many still believe in a foreign influx in the autumn—everything else he writes stands up well today. His views on the eyesight of wood pigeons are especially interesting:

> Numerous experiences suggest that when in flight pigeons see clearest a limited area of ground just in front, but are completely blind to what is below, comparatively blind sideways and do not see far ahead. If decoys are situated in the area of natural scrutiny they are less quick than ordinary to pick up any movement made by the shooter. When the latter is in a hide open at the top and an overhead approaching shot is taken at any angle of 45 degrees, they see the movement in time and swerve and give the oncoming charge a miss—a moment later their blind spot cuts you out. That a pigeon, at equally near range but crossing in front, seldom swerves confirms the theory that they are comparatively blind sideways.
>
> When a party of pigeons is seen to be likely to pass overhead, some of the above deductions may be turned to practical account. Confine your shooting to stragglers in the rear, then reload quickly because the main body will, on hearing the noise, break up in confusion to return in scattered fragments.

Not all pigeon shooters may agree with this. Max Baker's opinions are never less than interesting and mostly as sound as anything we know about the sport today.

Whatever else has changed, guns and cartridges have altered very little since pigeon shooting became Everyman's sport.

Archie Coats shot all his birds with a conventional side-by-side twelve-bore game gun. Some pigeon shooters prefer over-and-under twelve-bores in which one barrel is mounted above the other. It is a matter of choice.

For a long time it was believed that you needed big shot to kill pigeon. Number fours or fives were often advocated. The superstition that pigeons were hard to kill—and in my belief it was no better than a superstition—sprung from the fact that a wood pigeon is not only a very heavily-feathered bird but a very lightly-feathered one as well. A single pellet has only to flick across the breast, probably without doing any harm, for a whole cloud of feathers to be released on the wind. The bird flies away strongly and unharmed, and, unjustly earns itself the reputation of being armour-plated. It has to be admitted that a crop full of cabbage, say, can sometimes act as frontal armour! In fact, most decoy shooters use sixes and many, myself included, favour sevens. Most pigeons are killed over decoys within thirty yards. Within that range it is pattern that counts rather than the striking force of a few heavier pellets. Some experts manage to cut their cartridge bills by using one ounce loads such as IMI's Impax.

Hides? There is little doubt that a hide built in a hedge with a billhook out of natural materials, such as elder, is about as good as you can get. The most comfortable hide is made from sixteen or seventeen straw bales. (I even know one semi-professional who carries the materials for his own straw bale hide around on a trailer.) Farmers are not always keen to put bales out for pigeon shooters. In any case, bales may not be available. And if the farmer does drop off sixteen straw bales in a field, it likely that, with the best will in the world, he will deposit them in the wrong place!

Artificial hides were revolutionised by the Second World War, after which the MOD disposed of thousands of miles of surplus camouflage nets dressed with brown and green scrim. Originally intended for disguising tanks, vehicles and artillery pieces, these were equally good at hiding pigeon shooters. The only snag was that they were heavy, especially when wet. I still have one which I use as an underlayer on windy days when lighter hide material tends to flap in the breeze.

The shooting suppliers soon improved on the government patterns by producing lightweight nylon nets. You can fold up two of these, enough for a pigeon hide, and carry them in a game bag or even in the pockets of a shooting jacket. Their only snag is that they do tend to blow about in a gale, but it is a small matter to peg or weight them down.

Nowadays, all serious pigeon shooters have a set or two of hide poles. You can buy these ready-made, though I get mine made up by the blacksmith to my own specification. A set of six in varying lengths up to a maximum of six feet costs between £25 and £30. With nets draped from these you can quickly become invisible.

The area in which there is most room for experiment and improvement is that of artificial decoys. The shooting industry has produced many and varied patterns, as have individual shooters. I remember with a certain amount of affection those invented by David Home-Gall. You inflate the hollow plastic shell by blowing up a toy balloon inside the decoy. Fiddly work, but they look quite lifelike.

My first artificials were things of beauty but brutally heavy. They were made of wood. At one time I even had a museum piece from a bygone age made of cast iron. I have owned decoys you throw out from the hide like a boomerang, to simulate a pigeon landing. They should work but never seem to live up to their promise. I once built a balsa-wood pigeon glider that circled in front of the hide and landed fairly realistically, but it wasn't robust enough to stand the wear and tear. Then, there are commercially made shell decoys and full-bodied decoys in different postures. All of them on their day, and in favourable conditions, can pull the birds, but practically every one of them has a built-in snag. Their day is definitely not a sunny one. Wood pigeons know that their relatives' feathers do not gleam in the sunlight. I have only once or twice found a commercial artificial that is painted in sufficiently matt colours to look anything like the real article.

If like Lord Walsingham you have 'a willing and agile lad' handy you can get him to shin up and put a 'lofter' or two in the branches of a 'sitty' tree to attract passing birds. It works, but I never seem to have a lad who is sufficiently willing or agile to hand, and so, on the rare occasions I use this ruse, I employ telescopic lofting poles, which the shooting suppliers are happy to sell to enthusiasts. I am never clever enough to get the birds perching securely or even facing into the wind, the attitude in which every self-respecting pigeon sits, to avoid getting its feathers ruffled.

There is no doubt at all that dead birds make the best decoys. Failing that, artificials made to look as much as possible like dead birds. I often stick wings on my plastics though I don't go to the lengths of some experts I know who 'scalp' dead pigeons in order to glue their iridescent topknots on to dummies.

If you are shooting regularly, and killing a lot of pigeons, it pays to keep a dozen or two overnight to start off your decoy picture next day. Two days out in the field may not do these much good. Provided it is cool enough, I often bring the 'dirty dozen' in at the end of the second day and, provided they aren't too tatty, or, for that matter, 'chatty', I put aside their breasts for making pâté. A touch of gameyness adds to the flavour of the end result.

In the past, I have given a dozen or more dead birds heavy injections of formalin and then put them in the deep-freeze overnight so that they set in a lifelike feeding attitude. Once they have become set they do not need to be frozen again and do service for quite a long time.

In April 1994, John Humphreys, writing in his *Country Gun* page in *Shooting Times*, unearthed an interesting exhibit from a past age called the 'Bendecoy'. Ben, as John christened this object, was intended to be wired up to a car battery. When the gunner in his hide pressed a button, Ben arthritically flapped his metal wings.

There is no doubt that wing movement does attract, but it is a moot point whether Ben would be legal today. There are now strict rules about using mechanical aids in field sports. For instance, it is not legal to pursue and shoot wildfowl—and it certainly should not be—when using a motor-driven boat. Hand manipulation of decoys, though, is plainly within the rules. Many 'flappers' have been devised and put on the market, always with the object of activating the wings of a dead bird so that the white 'come hither' wing bars can flash their message to approaching or passing pigeons. Practically all of these are worked by pulling a cord. I have owned one or two but we have never got on well together, though I am sure the fault is on my side. Either the string catches in intervening foliage or vegetation, or the dog or I trip over the string when going out to retrieve or tidy up the decoy pattern.

The best of all movement devices at present is designed and marketed by John Batley, of Herefordshire, the only man I know who, at the moment of writing, makes his living either by shooting pigeons or teaching other people to shoot them.

The Batley pigeon cradles come in two models, 'The Incomer' and 'The Angel'. Both are mounted on highly-flexible metal poles. A long spike is passed through the dead bird's vent and up into its head. The wings are then supported on strong wire outriggers. The slightest breeze makes the pigeon sway and bob realistically on its metal rod. The 'Incomer' is mounted at the downwind end of the decoy pattern and the 'Angel', whose wings are in what I can only describe as the 'reverse thrust' attitude of a pigeon landing, at the upwind end. They are extraordinarily effective.

With all these aids and, despite the undoubted decoy-shyness of the modern wood pigeon, it is not surprising that the really skilled operators still make very large bags. Two Scottish keepers I know shot 780 pigeons in two days in Ayrshire last year. Only a month ago as I write, Jim Hackett of Surrey, with two friends, Rick Dean and Chris Jackson, shot 520 between 9.45 am and 7 pm on the Hog's Bag near Farnham and failed to pick a further eighty-five which fell in standing crops. Even then the birds were not coming to decoys but flighting to a field of laid barley one and a half miles away. Jim Hackett did not start shooting until midday. Had he been there from the start, the score would no doubt have been even higher. They fired 1,100 cartridges between them.

The ambition of the average pigeon shooter is to score one hundred in a day to his own gun. This is roughly the equivalent of making a century in a Test Match. John Batley, who has probably scored as many centuries as anyone, gives the following requirements for knocking up one hundred.

Rate of scoring is the most important. First, he says, ensure that you are under a flight-line. Many pigeon shooters don't make a sufficiently thorough recce. Have a comfortable hide and seat with your equipment decently stowed around you. You need a steady supply of pigeons, naturally, and you should be shooting two cartridges per bird or better. You can do it, he says, at three to one provided you don't stop for lunch or anything else. There are generally not more than five shooting hours in a pigeon day. You'll be firing at least two hundred cartridges. That's one shot every minute and a half. 'Shooting one hundred birds,' he adds, 'is hard work and physically demanding.'

If shooting a century is hard work—and I assure you it is—what can it be like shooting five times that number in a single day? No history of pigeon shooting would be complete without the story of how Archie Coats set the record and how John Ransford beat it eight years later. Here is Archie Coats' personal account of his big day from his book *Pigeon Shooting*.

My big pigeon shoot took place on 10th January, 1962, on Mr John Rowsell's farm at Stoke Charity on Lord Rank's estate. The field, sown with S.100 Aberystwyth clover for pigs, was no stranger to me and in 1961 we killed 800 or more pigeons off it in different shoots, the bale hide used being only a few yards from that used on my record day. I asked for some fresh bales to be put out and this was done some time in the first week of January. I set off about 9.30 am, meaning to shoot a clover ley on Lord Rank's manor farm at Micheldever. But I found the game shooting plans had been changed and so I could not go. I then went to have a look at Mr Rowsell's field as I knew I could shoot it, as 'first time over' for pheasants on that particular beat had taken place. This beat was in good form as that particular shoot was also a game record for the estate.

At the New Year we had had an intense period of cold and snow, and a great many pigeons had died. So I was not expecting an enormous bag and did not have as many cartridges in the van as I usually do. Also, my large bag with about a hundred cartridges in it had got wet the day before and had been forgotten as it was drying off. Anyway, the field was full of pigeons. I had luckily just caught the beat keeper, Mills, and got the OK to shoot. I was sure I was in for a 200 or more day.

It did not take me long to make the hide from the stack of bales and my little picture of ten birds was soon set out. I think I and Simba, my faithful yellow labrador, were in position at almost exactly 11 am. I had a 250 box to start with and about twenty-five in my small bag. And then they started and the first half hour was hot work, with three twenty-five boxes on the ledge open so that I could load from the top of each to save time and then empty one into the other. I think I picked up twice and got about seventy dead birds out as decoys, very few with heads propped up on sticks and the others simply propped up on the clover. After that it was not necessary to put birds out. They came without any lull from the two main lines of flight mostly; but there really were so many birds in the air over the decoys that I had to keep a tight rein, concentrate and observe a little hide discipline myself! Soon I had to go and get more cartridges. I went to the farm where I obtained 250. There were 500 there but I must say that I thought 250 would be enough. About half way through these, I had to alter my opinion and realised for the first time that if I went on at that rate, I could beat the existing record, though I was not certain what that was—anyway I knew it was not more than 500. I had a short tidy up though I could not possibly control the feathers and the place was looking rather like a plucking shed. Then I ran out again at about 2 pm. By this time, poor Simba looked as if he was suffering from shell shock though he had not had much to do. I took him back to the car. I then drove to the farm again. The office was shut! I was desperately looking for someone who had a key, when luckily Mr Rowsell's secretary appeared. It was just as well, as I meant to have that box of 250 somehow. On the way back, I met Mills who was watching and told him I hoped to beat the record. He kindly volunteered to come and spot for me in the hide. This he did, bringing a young labrador with him. By this time, I had lowered the front bale so that we were practically in full view of the birds. It made no difference. The muscles of my thighs were very sore from getting up for certain shots so I decided to shoot entirely sitting down which was easy enough as birds were always on the decoys and some even turned back when they had just been shot at. Otherwise, I was not really tired, only anxious to beat the record and have done. They really went for the decoys and for about twenty minutes the gun was uncomfortably hot to hold, though I was wearing mittens. It was very hot most of the time, but this period, I think, was the quickest.

After this, Mills did a count of sorts though it was very difficult and made the score over 500. By this time it was about 3.15 pm and there was a slight slackening off. So I decided to enjoy myself, taking everything at any angle and then to stop at 4 pm. By this time the word had spread and I fear John Rowsell lost a few man-hours, there being quite an audience.

The last ten minutes were relatively quiet and I stopped shooting at 4 pm and relaxed, though not looking forward to the appalling task of picking up, there being towered birds all over the field. Luckily I was able to borrow a few sacks and drive the van right up to the hide. While I hunted Simba all over the field, Mills and a helper put the slain around the hide in piles of 50. Needless to say, I did not hunt any of the surrounding strips as a second (pheasant) shoot was soon to come on that beat and the birds would soon be going up to roost. Despite the cannonade, several pheasants fed in the field during the day.

We sacked exactly 550 pigeons at the hide. There were 125 cartridges left out of the last 250 box so I used about 650. Altogether I must have wasted about forty minutes shooting time getting cartridges, so my arithmetic makes this one pigeon every 28.5 seconds and one shot every 24 seconds. So I suppose I could have broken 600 carrying the normal amount of cartridges in the van and still leaving enough time to get one lot from the farm. Perhaps the best thing of the day was that Mills only picked up seven the next day when feeding the strips, but the pigs may have had a few.

If you do anything professionally for long enough you will hit the jackpot sooner or later. I expect if you fish a river for many years in all weathers and get to know the lies and the water really well you may one day kill fifty salmon in a day. Anyway, I don't want to do it again and good luck to anyone who breaks this score. But I will lay odds that he will have to use a bale hide to do it!

Eight years later, John Ransford, who runs some very excellent pheasant shoots in the Welshpool area and along the Welsh border, beat Archie's record, though he certainly didn't set out with that object in mind. John and his father have been shooting very large bags of pigeon for years. I am indebted to John Ransford and to the editor of *Shooting Times* for permission to quote from his story:

From early July, I noticed pigeon feeding on a sixteen-acre field of wheat alongside the main road. Two or three times each week, I passed this field and always stopped and clapped my hands to see what number of pigeon would rise from the areas which were laid. Each time, between 50 and 150 rose. I felt they were not really worth bothering about. Also, all the laid corn was in the middle of the field and it would have been difficult to make a hide. Each time, I noticed that the farmer had hung more coloured polythene bags about the field until the whole of the laid area looked like a fairground. Nevertheless, some pigeon continued to use the field.

The farmer telephoned me a number of times and asked me to shoot them. After the third request, I suggested that he cleared all the coloured bags and the automatic bird scarer from the field and put seventeen straw bales in the middle.

On Wednesday, 22 July, I arrived at the farm about 1.30 pm and immediately saw a considerable number of birds using the field. The farmer was on holiday but two of his men helped me to carry my decoys and cartridges to the heap of bales. I quickly made a very comfortable hide and left one bale to sit on. I always take trouble putting out my decoys and I was able to set them out in such a way that the decoyed birds would come head on to the hide.

There was a very strong wind blowing although it was a bright sunny day. Before the men went back to their work, they took the Land Rover and put scarecrows on adjoining fields of wheat where a few pigeon had been feeding. One was placed on the far side of the actual field I was in. This prevented any birds settling before they saw the decoys.

Immediately I was in the hide and before I had loaded my gun, pigeon were over the decoys and well in the killing area. In the first half hour of shooting, I fired 100 cartridges from my bag. In the following hour, I fired a 250 boxful.

By this time, one of the farm men had arrived and I immediately sent him to collect another 500 cartridges from the Land Rover. He came and sat in the hide and loaded for me, for now the barrels of both guns were becoming unpleasantly warm.

The pigeon using this particular field were travelling considerable distances. The previous day, my father had shot 170 pigeon on the same estate and had noticed a continual stream of birds flying high over his decoys obviously making for this field of wheat a mile down the valley.

Nearly every pigeon that came to the field decoyed, many dropping from a great height. The continual shooting never deterred them in the slightest degree as a strong wind muffled the sound of the shots. Pigeon were in the air the whole time, coming from all directions, the wind guiding them to the decoys.

By about six o'clock the whole of the decoying area looked like a blue and white carpet with the dead birds lying in all positions. This did not alarm those which were still coming in. However, I did use my fully choked gun most of the last two hours because the decoyed birds were circling very wide and many were shot at over forty yards.

I finally stopped shooting at 6.50 pm, having fired 699 cartridges. Just as I finished, a friend, Bryan Owen, and his brother returned to help me pick up along with a farmer's son from a nearby farm who had heard the continual shooting.

Before we began to collect the dead birds, we picked up the decoys, many of which had been knocked over by the falling pigeon. In the immediate area in front of the hide we picked up 469 pigeon before I allowed the dogs to work.

I drove the Land Rover into the field to save the long carry to the hedge with the dead birds, etc. While I was away, the other men circled the adjoining field and looked under every tree and bush for birds which had left the shooting area wounded. They returned with over 40 birds.

For over an hour I worked the dogs sytematically round and round the hide through the standing wheat. I always find that dead pigeon which fall into standing grain are very difficult to find even with very experienced dogs.

Whenever I shoot pigeon over standing corn, I keep an accurate count of kills and misses, putting the empty cartridge cases in separate bags. After counting the empty cases I was fairly certain that I had killed just over 600 pigeon but at one time during the afternoon the shooting was so rapid that it was difficult to direct the empty cases into the correct hit or miss bags.

Before the final pick-up was complete, the head keeper arrived and helped to bag and count the dead birds. The final pick-up was 561. There were only five stock doves in this very large bag. On the following days the farm men noticed odd dead pigeon under trees on other parts of the farm.

During the past two years I have noticed an increase in the number of pigeon in this area, the Shropshire-Montgomeryshire border. In February and March this year we shot very large numbers of pigeon coming to roost in various woods. One evening I shot ninety-seven in three quarters of an hour. In July this year we shot 2,403 pigeon in ten days—and not even shooting all day at that!

Archie Coats was shooting in Hampshire, John Ransford in Shropshire, both first-rate pigeon areas. As Coats predicted, John Ransford beat his total from the comfort of a bale hide!

On Sunday 25 June, 1994, John Ransford's twenty-four-year-old record was beaten by two birds by twenty-six-year-old Andrew Atkinson shooting on fifty acres of set-aside at Bourne in Lincolnshire. The attraction was self-seeded barley. Andrew shot between 8 am and 8.30 pm. He started in a bale hide but after some time decided the pigeons felt uneasy about it and moved to a net hide in the bottom of a dry ditch. Like the previous record-holders he had no intention of attempting a record score. He knew that there were a lot of pigeons using the field and hoped to top his previous best of 178 to his own gun. The record will undoubtedly be broken again. Apart from the ability to shoot pigeons, whoever does it will need an awful lot of pigeons and the ideal conditions. Like his predecessors he will almost certainly break the record without setting out to do so.

Since Andrew Atkinson broke the record on set-aside land, perhaps this is the point at which to add a note on the importance of the set-aside policy to the pigeon-shooter. I asked Mike Swan of the Game Conservancy Advisory Service for his views on the subject. He told me:

Some farmers are using the Wild Bird Cover option to provide extra winter cover for game and wildlife. This can give rise to little patches of kale mixtures which provide hard weather food for pigeon and therefore opportunities for pigeon shooters.

Set-aside provides two main areas of interest to decoy shooters. First, more cereal and rape stubbles are being left over winter to regenerate naturally. Grains spilt on these after the harvest can draw birds and later on there can be new growth from these grains. Weeds, especially chickweed which pigeons love, are also likely to appear on set-aside land.

Secondly, set-aside rules allow non-agricultural crops such as industrial rape and linseed to be grown. If you have the only field growing one of these crops in your parish, then the sporting potential can be very great.

7

The Master

IN THE story of the wood pigeon two great names stand out. In some ways, they are, or rather were, opposed to each other. In others they saw eye to eye, though there did not seem to be much common ground at the time. I have already written about Ron Murton at some length. Now, it is the turn of that other great figure, Archie Coats. Archie, a dear and great friend, was the finest pigeon shooter of all time. Through his writings and lectures he taught a whole generation, in fact several generations, the art and skills of pigeon shooting. There can be little doubt that he was instrumental in altering some of the habits of that remarkably adaptable bird. Through his teachings, so many of us became skilful at the solitary art of hide shooting that wood pigeons throughout the land have grown considerably more suspicious about, and wary of, decoys.

I believe that I was originally responsible for christening Archie 'The Master'. The soubriquet has stuck. Use the description in informed shooting circles and no one has any doubt about whom you are talking. In his peak years, in the late 1950s, he was shooting around 25,000 pigeons a year and averaging sixty-five per cent, though the true score was more likely to have been nearer seventy-five per cent. Archie shot pigeons on some of the finest game-shooting estates in the south of England. He was punctilious, when it came to picking up, in avoiding nesting cover in the breeding season and coverts the keeper was nursing for 'the next time over'. It was inevitable therefore that a fair percentage of his kills remained ungathered.

His methods and techniques have been learned by many, including the writer, who was lucky enough to shoot with the Master on many occasions. In fact, I was touched, when going through the papers which his widow, Prue Coats, so kindly made available to me, to find that my name was included in his 'First Eleven'. In fact, the team in question was his *second* 'First Eleven'. Most of the original 'First' had, by the time of my own inclusion, retired or passed on. Will Garfit, illustrator of this book, was also in our team—flattering company to share, since I regard Will as one of the finest all-round shots in the land. To be included in the magic 'First Eleven' you had to be able to average at least two to one and preferably far better or you would draw the Master's fire. Worse still, you might find him sharing your hide. The Master's language, should you fall from grace, was terrible to hear. Archie was, however, the kindest of men, the original paper tiger. He might huff and puff but would never blow the fragile house of your self-esteem down. If you could shoot pigeons two to one with the Master spotting for you and offering criticism and advice from the back of your hide, you truly deserved your first eleven colours.

Here I am concerned not so much with his techniques as with the man himself. Nothing about A. Coats, including his way of life, was routine, though the facts of his career outside pigeon shooting are known to very few people.

Archie was born in 1916 and brought up in Sundrum Castle, Ayrshire. His family bore a name famous, still famous, in the cotton and textile industry. Archie, the youngest of seven, was in his wife Prue's words, 'the runt of the litter'. Family photographs of his five brothers and one sister bear this out. What he lacked in stature compared with his siblings he more than made up in good looks, a blessing he was to put to full use in his romantic life. Women frequently found him devastating.

His parents, however, were not quite so devastated at the way the youngest of the family was developing. Like his brothers he had a gun or fishing rod in his hands from a very early age. His country leanings would have been fine if they had stopped there. He was sent to Eton to prepare him for entering the family firm. However, he much preferred keeping hawks and shooting duck and snipe at the local sewage farm to studies designed to train him for commerce. It was when he let the family know that, when he left school, he wished to be a land agent, or factor as the role is known in Scotland, that the feathers, so to speak, hit the fan. This was a distinctly *infra dig* ambition, not at all in keeping with the Coats family traditions.

When he left Eton in 1934, his parents sent him to Paris to learn French, still in the hope that he would make a pillar of the family firm. He learned the language most successfully and much else besides, including *haute cuisine*, winning a certificate from a high-class French school of cookery for cooking meat and making sauces. This, like most Archie experiences of that era, had its romantic side. He had quickly acquired an attractive French girlfriend who was taking a cookery course. The only way he could see her regularly was by enlisting on the course himself.

From Paris, he was sent to gain experience in the Coats thread mills in Czechoslovakia, Hungary and Poland— shooting and breaking hearts with equal skill along the way. Pictures of him in Munich, where he stayed with a family called Romberg to learn German, reveal him dinner-jacketed, white-tied and every sartorial inch what Prue describes in that thoroughly period phrase 'a positive debs' delight'.

A sinister note creeps into his German stay. The Coats family was extremely well connected and it may be through one of those connections—though the family firm would certainly not have approved—that Archie was persuaded to help influential Jews leave Hitler's Germany. For this undercover work, he was recruited by Sir Noel Mason McFarlane, a high-ranking member of the Diplomatic Service. It was a job that these days would probably be given to someone professionally trained in such dangerous work. The Gestapo got wind of Archie's activities, arrested him and under interrogation beat him up with rubber truncheons. The damage done to the muscles in his buttocks during those beatings was to play a fateful part in his professional pigeon shooting life forty-two years later.

The encounter with the German forces of law and order— if you could thus describe the Gestapo of 1939—did not go down well with the Coats family. They saw the encounter in commercial terms, as something that might adversely affect their trade relationships with Nazi Germany.

Archie merely extended his diplomatic connections in another direction, falling for Virginia de Ferranti di Ruffino, the extremely beautiful daughter of the Italian consul in Frankfurt. Her mother was an American and a cousin of the Vanderbilts. Archie married her. War broke out soon after. When Italy declared war, Archie found himself with a father-in-law on the other side. By then Archie had enlisted in the Scots Guards and Virginia, through her mother's connections, had moved to America.

Coats' war record was as rich and varied as any other part of his life, perhaps more so. An Italian bomb winged him badly at the first battle of Sidi Rezegh in 1941. When he recovered from his wounds, he was seconded to the Equatorial Battalion of the Sudan Defence Force.

I recall Archie's own account of that service. It went more-or-less as follows. 'When I found I was expected to patrol about 1,200 miles of frontier with one battalion, I looked around for something useful I could do. The locals asked me if I could do something about controlling the elephants that were raiding their shambas. I like jumbos, but plainly I had to oblige. After I had shot the first bull and it had trundled on and collapsed nearly on top of me I realised that shooting elephants with a .303 service rifle *just was not on.*'

I treasure those last four words as a classic item of Coats understatement. A faded photograph shows how close that bull elephant came to achieving what the Italian air force had failed to do. Both frontal and brain shots on an elephant need to be placed with almost surgical precision to guarantee a clean kill. For a lightly jacketed .303 round to have done the job at all, Coats must have shot, as always, with considerable accuracy. A Lee Enfield service rifle is just not enough gun. Archie was the first to realise this. I found a letter from him addressed to the District Commissioner asking permission to purchase a .475 Rigby big game rifle for £50, permission that was happily granted.

Service on the Sudan frontier was not entirely confined to elephant control. I found some notes about an undercover operation carried out by Coats and his men to lay flares inside Italian territory to guide British bombers to their target.

In the autumn of 1943 Archie was appointed personal assistant to Dick Casey, British Minister of State in the Middle East. In this role he was present at both the Cairo and Teheran Conferences. At one of these, the general outline of 'Operation Overlord', the coming invasion of Europe, had been discussed. Some details had been chalked up on the blackboard. Churchill had just suggested that the press could now be allowed in for a briefing—but not, of course, about Overlord—when Archie realised that the blackboard notes had not been wiped away. So he had to stand up and stop the great man in mid-flow and suggest the press be held while the blackboard was cleaned. I gather that interrupting Churchill made even young Captain Coats take a deep breath. Major Coats ended a varied and distinguished war—some said he should have been decorated for the operation laying flares behind Italian lines in the Sudan—as an instructor at Sandhurst.

The family took a rather less jaundiced view of 'The Major' after he was demobbed. The firm took him back and sent him to America where he created a minor stir at Grand Central Station, New York, by commuting daily in bowler hat and rolled umbrella. But he hated the office work and his marriage, which had produced one son and two daughters, was sadly breaking down. He returned to England in 1949 without a job, until a brother officer invited him to spend a year culling deer on his Scottish estate. Another romantic entanglement put an end to that arrangement. He came back to London and lived in the Guards Club.

Then, in 1950, he met Prue, who was working for the British Bloodstock Agency, and instantly earned the total disapproval of her family. He was, after all, still married to his Italian-American wife and was out of work. Prue was, however, the best thing that had happened to Archie and vice-versa. Despite the fact that her parents disapproved, even when Archie's divorce came through, they did come to the wedding in 1952, though on the way in the car Prue's mother said to her: 'There's still time to change your mind, dear.'

As a sop to his wife's parents, Archie took a job with an export-import firm. One day he came home and said: 'I don't think I can stand it any longer. Would you mind if I became

a full-time pigeon shooter?' Prue, of course, said: 'No, go
ahead,' even though her parents refused to speak to him for a
long time as a result of this decision.

While he had been instructing at Sandhurst at the end of the
war, Archie had spent his weekends shooting pigeons in the
Hampshire and Berkshire countryside, selling the bag to a
protein-starved public in order to pay his hotel bills. The
germ of the idea for his eventual career had been sown during
these expeditions. For six months, the newly-married Coats
lived in London, camping and shooting pigeons at weekends,
mostly on Lord Rank's estate at Sutton Scotney but also
along the Hog's Back. During the winter of 1952, they moved
to the Deane Gate Inn at Deane, where they paid a reduced
rate in return for washing up when the bar closed. It helped
that the landlord was a formidable pigeon gun himself.

They eventually found lodgings in a two-up-two-down
called 'Landi Khotal' in the Hampshire village of Dummer.
Prue remembers this period as being 'fairly squalid and very
damp'. Her one Paquin dress developed a coating of green
mould. Tower Hill Farm became their happy home and the
centre of the Coats pigeon industry, with ten acres, in 1954,
for £4,000.

Archie was now well launched on a career which, I have
always maintained, made him one of the most successful and
happiest men I have ever known. He carved a way of life that
he loved out of what many people, including parents and
relations on both sides, saw as a non-starter.

To give themselves a foundation on which to build, Archie
persuaded Lord Rank of Sutton Scotney to pay him £1,000 a
year to shoot pigeons on crops seven days a week, three
hundred and sixty five days a year (if necessary). Another big
landowner who might have profited equally in terms of
protected crops, huffily turned down Archie's proposal as he
thought gentlemen did not shoot for money! Archie was
nevertheless retained to protect in all 17,000 acres, though in
those early days he shot over a total of 65,000, most of them
without direct support from the farmers, though sometimes
obtaining free or reduced cartridges and occasionally 'petrol
money'. Between them, Archie and Prue thought up sidelines.

They grew Christmas trees on part of the ten acres until Selfridges, to whom they also supplied oven-ready pigeons, started selling plastic trees and knocked them out of business. Then it was *fraises du bois* for the Savoy Hotel group. The ladies from the village who came in to pluck and prepare pigeons also helped with the strawberry picking. In 1960 the Coats also became game dealers.

It was often a fairly precarious business. From 1949 to 1961, Prue also worked for Tom Gullick (one of Archie's original First Eleven and later to be the 'emperor' of driven partridge shooting in Spain). Tom was then becoming a big-wheel in the travel business, organising tulip flights to Holland for Clarksons, the travel firm he had revolutionised. I mention this because after the disastrous freezing winter of 1962-63, when pigeons became thin on the ground, Archie (adept in several languages) took a job as a courier with Tom Gullick's firm. He got the push from his old friend for taking Prue out to dinner in Madrid and neglecting the high-ranking American officers' wives he was supposed to be showing round the city. Tom and Archie, however, remained the greatest of friends despite this typical hiccup. Making a living was now even more important. In 1961, Prue produced a daughter, Lucy, who not surprisingly turned out to be an excellent beater, stop and all-round shooting man's aid and supporter, the apple of Archie's eye.

In spite of the varied supporting and ancillary activities, Archie's mainstay was always shooting pigeons. From the start, he was deeply involved in what might be called the politics of the wood pigeon. Killing the bird in large numbers and thus protecting farmers' crops was his livelihood. This livelihood was perpetually threatened in one way or another. The threats came from the excessively hard winter weather, from scientific research, and from bumbling and uninformed civil servants. The latter were particularly troublesome. Archie argued—though from a standpoint quite different from Dr Murton's—that the mass roosting shoots were largely a waste of time and ammunition. Shooting over some 17,000 acres of Hampshire and Berkshire, Archie knew what could be achieved by a skilled decoy shooter. As early as August 1953, he was lobbying a fellow shooting man and old companion from wartime days, Christopher Soames MP, to get him an interview with 'someone really high up in the Min of Ag who understands what I am talking about'.

'Some time ago,' he wrote to Soames, 'I went to Tolworth, Ministry of Agriculture Pest Control HQ. I wanted to put up a scheme with which every pest officer in Hants, Surrey, Berks, Wilts and Beds agrees.'

The scheme called for a cadre of trained decoy shooters in the prime pigeon counties, paid for by the farmers and subsidised by the Ministry. Archie himself would be willing to train this élite force. To start with, there would be one expert pigeon gun in each of the hardest-hit counties who in turn would train others as necessary. At Tolworth he found himself engaged in what is sometimes described in agricultural metaphor as 'kicking a sack of wheat'. ('Try it sometime. You are liable to break a toe.') Characteristically, Archie was more likely to have described it as 'kicking against the pricks'. To Soames he wrote:

> The pest people would not look at it, and I realised they were quite ignorant of the problem. The man I saw did not even know that you could shoot pigeons with decoys on their feeding grounds in daylight!! On his door was the legend '2 I/C Feathered Pest, UK'. So I gave it up.
>
> They have now gone ahead with the cheap cartridges for 'organised shoots' but today I am informed by the local pest officer that only No. 4 shot is being issued by ICI. Doubtless, they have a surplus of 4s and this is a heaven-sent opportunity to get rid of them. You know as well as I do that 4s are quite useless for pigeon except under very special conditions.

He was still hammering away, without success and without an issue of Ministry-subsidised cartridges seven years later, though he had managed to get the shot size decreased to 5s and 6s—though the ideal shot size is, for my money, No. 7. It is pattern that counts when shooting over decoys.

Using a standard twelve-bore game gun, Archie was firing at least 30,000 cartridges a year. He was forced to rely on what he could get through Rabbit Clearance Societies and supporting farmers, though very few of the latter were willing to subsidise the protection he gave them. In 1969, the Rabbit Clearance Societies and the half-price cartridge scheme were wound up. A pigeon in the feather then fetched one shilling from a game dealer—if you were lucky. The Coats cottage industry subsequently started oven-readying some of the bag and selling nicely-packed pigeons to some of the big London stores.

During this lean period, Prue worked for Tom Gullick organising Clarkson's tulip flights to Holland. Archie advised on several big shoots in Austria and there were always Germans, Scandinavians and Dutch at Tower Hill, willing to pay generously for the splendid fare provided by Prue and the marvellous pigeon shooting arranged by the Master. Life was often precarious but it was never dull.

I can remember a time in the late 1950s when Archie had a personal 'hit list'. High on it were Wedgie Benn and Dr Ron Murton, both of whom he saw as a threat to his way of life, Benn, presumably, because of his well-known lack of sympathy with field sports; Ron Murton for his views on the non-effectiveness of pigeon control by shooting. Murton's experiments at Carlton and elsewhere in controlling pigeons by the use of narcotics were, if successful, obviously a direct threat to a professional pigeon shooter. There was also a potential knock-on effect. Once the eating public got the idea that pigeons were being 'poisoned', the market in their flesh would fall as dramatically as that of rabbits after myxomatosis. Archie and Murton did meet 'over a table' to discuss these issues, however, and there must have been a partial rapport between them, as among Archie's documents are several of Dr Murton's newly-published papers inscribed 'with compliments, R.K. Murton'.

The third enemy was the weather. In 1962–3 it struck with the worst winter in living memory, with disastrous results on the pigeon population. Like all dedicated pigeon shooters, Archie had a total respect for his quarry. (If any non-shooters read these words, they may find this basic 'hunting' truth hard to accept.)

I do not remember [he wrote] how long that winter lasted but it was certainly one of the hardest in the last century. The effect not only on pigeons but all birds was catastrophic. Towards the end, it was not worth shooting pigeons. Nature was doing the job far more efficiently. You could go up any hedgerow bordering kale or brassicas and find them lying dead—and this is no exaggeration—by the score. I never want to see anything like it again.

Pigeon shooting, day in day out, is extremely hard work. Apart from the sheer physical effort of humping gear, setting out decoys, discharging a twelve-bore perhaps a hundred times in four or five hours, bagging the slain and carrying the gear off at the end of the day, there is the sheer mental concentration needed. The moment one relaxes, there is a bird you never spotted over the decoys.

In the late 1970s, Archie began to suffer from hip trouble. In view of the hours he spent crouched in a hide or carrying heavy loads across all manner of rough terrain from sticky plough to brick-hard stubbles, this was not really surprising. Hip operations are successful for ninety-nine per cent of those who have artificial joints fitted. In 1981 Archie had one hip done but the artificial joint had to be removed as it had not taken. The surgeons told him that the beating up he had taken at the hands of the Gestapo in 1939 had so knotted the muscles in his buttocks that the plastic joint could not do its job. The remaining hip could not be operated on and was extremely arthritic and painful to use. From then on, he had to get around on worn-out bone and cartilage and a pair of metal sticks. It must have been agony much of the time.

Though he shot less frequently, he was still out two, three or four days a week, shooting as straight as ever. The SAS, members of whom sometimes shot with him, made him a special swivelling seat. (One SAS officer who spent his week's leave with the Master in the field declared he was quite pleased to go back to duty for a rest cure.)

But the weight, quite literally, fell on his loving wife Prue, who took him out every morning, set him up in his hide (obeying like any other acolyte a string of instructions which she knew by heart). She helped put out his decoys, visited him at least once during the day to see if he needed moving and finally picked up at the end of the day and brought him home.

Prue knew perfectly well that any other way of life was unthinkable for him and that he would have died if he had had to sit around the house all day (and so, probably, would anyone else who was in range).

Towards the end, I remember coming home after a long day in the field. Archie was hobbling on his sticks into Tower Hill Farm, for a large *boisson*—drinks were quite often referred to in French.

We had unloaded the gear and laid out the pigeons in the cooler, and were following the Master into the house. The rear view was remarkable. From hat to shoes he looked like something that grew in a hedgerow. I swear his shooting jackets changed their cropping and colour with the seasons and that real vegetation grew on them. The trousers draped round the now largely-useless legs were crinkled and hung in grey folds.

'Look at him,' Prue said. 'He looks just like a ****ing old elephant.' I have seldom heard a wifely description more lovingly made.

Not long after this, Archie returned from a day shooting pigeons, sat by the fire with a large *boisson* in hand, phoned up a friend about arranging some shooting for the next day, and died. He was seventy-three.

As this book will have made clear there is considerable doubt, to say the least, about whether shooting can ever really affect the numbers of wood pigeon in Britain. Whatever the eventual findings of the scientists examining this aspect of the pigeon problem, there can be no doubt about one thing. Throughout his career, Archie Coats made a considerable impression on the pigeon population of the Home Counties, Hampshire and Berkshire in particular. Whatever this did, or did not do, to the total population it is clear that his efforts saved many hundreds of thousands of pounds of crops. I have managed to salvage from the records his bag figures between 1954, when he started as a professional, until 1980. The record is not complete since he continued shooting several days a week right up until his death. Here is the tally, as far as it goes:

Between 1954 and 1964 he picked up (perhaps ten per cent fewer than he actually shot) 165,000 pigeons. As I have already said, the big years were the late 1950s when he shot as many as 25,000 in twelve months. The record between 1960 and 1980 is as follows:

1960	3,518	1967	3,692	1974	4,166
1961	7,366	1968	2,560	1975	5,799
1962	3,583	1969	3,993	1976	2,340
1963	1,544	1970	3,387	1977	7,225
1964	6,665	1971	2,389	1978	5,850
1965	4,918	1972	4,089	1979	6,258
1966	6,990	1973	4,698	1980	4,150
				Total:	95,180

There is, of course, a four year overlap between these figures, which I found in the Game Conservancy files, and his own total of 165,000 for his first ten years as a full-time professional. From the 1980s onwards he was suffering from hip trouble and was not shooting as heavily or quite as often. So if we add these two totals together (taking into account the four year overlap) we arrive at a total of over a quarter of a million pigeons. I doubt whether it has been equalled since or for that matter ever will be equalled, let alone surpassed.

These are the bare facts of a remarkable man and a remarkable life, but perhaps they don't quite give the entire picture. I hope this extract from my own shooting diary gives some flavour of a day out with the pigeons as the Master's pupil:

April 10. 1976. A phone call from Archie. They are drilling some wheat at Sutton Scotney. Pigeons should be on to it the day after tomorrow. Phone tomorrow night for final orders. Archie's First Eleven know this routine well. Within twenty-four hours the pigeon situation can have become what the Master describes as 'a major disaster'. 'My dear boy, there's been a major disaster they've all ✱✱✱✱ed off to Essex for the peas' .... 'The bloody man [the farmer] hasn't drilled his wheat as he said he would ....' etc, etc.

There are endless combinations and permutations of major disasterdom. So much so, that Coats, known locally as 'the Major', is often referred to by his close pigeon shooting friends as 'Major Disaster'. But this time, not. A phone call establishes that the field has not only been drilled but that the pigeons have found it. 'Be here by eight-thirty sharp. No. Better come for breakfast.'

So I turn up at seven-thirty and at nine we are still loading gear into the battered van. Sutton Scotney belongs to Lord Rank. It is perhaps Archie's first priority. He is paid to defend it, and defend it he does, though never without full consultation with head keepers, beat keepers and anyone else whose work might be affected by his shooting.

Despite the fact that the decibel level in his venerable van is about equal to that experienced when flying in an open cockpit, Archie talks round the stem of the pipe clamped in his mouth all the way. We are both gun-deaf so neither of us hears much or expects to hear much. My routine replies possibly have no revelance to the questions and remarks that occasioned them.

There are quite a few birds on the drills when we arrive. Archie knows every inch of this ground and the behaviour of pigeons in almost any wind, weather and on any likely crop. Despite this, he is not satisfied with a prospect that would please the average pigeon shooter exceedingly.

When you have shot with the Master for some years, you realise that he is right to be doubtful. You resign yourself and tell your trigger finger to stop itching. You are going to look at every other possible alternative target for the pigeons that day. As befits an ex-Scots Guards officer and Sandhurst instructor, Archie believes implicitly in the old army axiom: 'Time spent in reconnaissance is seldom wasted.'

We only spend half an hour this time glassing various fields, sitting watching flight-lines in and out of woods, until Coats says: 'That's it then, boy.' Almost every pigeon shooting companion of any age is addressed as 'boy'.

I am to shoot on the drilled wheat. Archie will set up on a smaller pea field half a mile away. He judges that the noise of our gunfire, what he calls 'the power of shot', will keep the birds on the move to the benefit of us both.

After more than ten years apprenticeship, he grudgingly admits that I can be trusted to build my own hide—in this case nets and stakes recessed into the elder bushes in a long narrow shelter belt of trees. He will even allow that I can set out my decoy picture fairly convincingly, though he may grunt and growl a bit and move one or two of the lures more to his liking.

I know full well that, as he drives away in his ancient vehicle, if he doesn't hear much shooting—and probably even if he does—he will be back in an hour or two to tell me what I am doing wrong. It's bound to be my fault, not the pigeons.

Nothing happens for nearly an hour and a half. Another Archie dictum is: 'If they don't come back in half an hour, something's wrong, boy.' But this time he was utterly confident that they would come back and I have learned to believe him. The first pigeon comes in, but I am asleep and miss it with both barrels. Two or three shots from the pea field half a mile away upwind. The power of shot is getting things moving. Three birds arrive together, almost before I have seen them. I shoot one on the ground and a second as it takes off—the correct drill. When you need dead birds to build up a decoy picture, you don't scruple about bumping them as sitters. The Master's words again: 'You're here to shoot pigeons, boy.'

When I see the dread vehicle appearing at half-past one I have twenty-two slain out, their heads pegged up on six inch twigs cut from the hedge to look more like the genuine article.

The Master grudgingly admits that I don't seem to be doing too badly but he swears he could see my face above the top of the nets as he drove up. 'Hide discipline, boy!'

The pigeons start to taper off around four-thirty. By that time, I have seventy and the Master another fifty-five. He talks all the way home and I reply, but as usual neither of us has heard a word the other has said. It's all been about the day, of course, so probably we were talking more or less about the same things. We unload the bag back at Tower Hill Farm and lay the birds, breast upwards, to cool. Tomorrow the ladies from the village will pluck and oven-ready the best of them. They are all as plump as they should be on spring sowings. 'A *boisson*, my boy.' *Boisson* in hand, we compare notes on what for me has been a great day and for Archie an average one. Almost for the first time that day, we can carry on a conversation that makes sense to both of us. I will be back at work tomorrow. So will Archie, on the drilled wheat, or the peas, and the day after that, and the day after that, and so on *ad infinitum*. Not sure that I would last the pace myself.

8

A Wood Pigeon Almanac

I HAVE kept a shooting diary since 1962. In it, often in the briefest note form, is a record of every time I have taken my gun out of the cabinet, even if only to stroll down a hedgerow with a spaniel for half an hour. Wildfowling, rough shooting, driven game shooting, even the occasional grouse shooting; they are all recorded there. I have left pigeon shooting until last. I started to count the number of times in those thirty odd years I had set up a hide, crouched in a ditch or stood in a roosting wood at dusk. I gave up when I had reached a thousand pigeon expeditions, though there was still a year or two to be reckoned with.

Most of the pigeon days accounted for fewer than twenty birds. Not a few were blanks. There were some notable one hundred-plus days, though most of these occured over ten years ago. It is increasingly difficult to knock up a century now, for reasons which I have already touched upon; for one thing we have made the birds smarter. And, of course, they diary includes a handful of red-letter days when the bag topped the one hundred and fifty mark.

Blank days, single figure days, average days, exceptional days; I cannot recall one that has not taught me something about the wood pigeon or illustrated some aspect of its behaviour.

I said in my introduction that this was not primarily a shooting book. Nor it is. So, in recreating a handful of days from my shooting diaries throughout the year I am compiling a brief wood pigeon almanac, hoping to show what the birds may be feeding on in any given month, how they behaved in different circumstances, and every now and again, for light relief, how I behaved—not invariably creditably.

January

January 13th, 1963. My birthday, so reckon I am entitled to go and look for some pigeons. This exceptionally hard weather has put them on any greenstuff they can find above snow level. Having to earn a living is a nuisance. I haven't been able to get at them for a week. The last lot I shot on turnip tops were in fair condition but, if they've switched to kale because the snow has deepened, they will be in miserable shape. Kale seems to go right through them without touching the sides!

Went to the Southwood Manor nursery farm, Surrey, to find a handful of birds on what remained of the turnip tops (mostly buried by snow). Twenty plus rose from a small plot of 'primo' cabbage behind the owner's house. One or two were reluctant to leave and sat tight pecking the cabbage tops even when I drove into the field. The cabbages are taking heavy punishment so the nurseryman will probably put up with a cannonade in his back garden if it's likely to help save his crop.

Wonderful, crisp, sub-zero day with bright blue sky and little wind. Not ideal by any means. Set a dozen decoys out on snow in clear space and perched a couple on top of cabbages. Put up net hide behind house in hedge.

First birds came at once, skimming in low, totally ignoring the decoys and heading for badly bashed cabbages twenty yards to the left. Dropped them with an easy left and right and set them out as extra decoys.

I needn't have bothered. Birds kept coming to the same patch of cabbage as if it was the only thing to eat for miles around. Perhaps it was! Shot thirty in the first hour. Had to go home for more cartridges. Ended with fifty-five by lunch time. Surprisingly, most of the pigeons were in reasonable condition though the breasts on a couple were as thin as razor blades.

NOTE: *I should have known that decoys don't work on snow. Despite their incredible eyesight, wood pigeons appear not to be able to see them against the white background. Presume they must be dazzled. Have found birds will sometimes fly directly overhead when I am out in the open. This is when they are heading into bright sunlight or even a low sun. This, surely, reinforces the dazzle theory.*

February

February 6th, 1963. Roosting at Bagnor in Berkshire with Jack Hargreaves in wood belonging to Billy Wallace, Princess Margaret's friend. Too still and not enough guns out to shift the birds around. Really do doubt the value of these mass roost shoots. Usually lots of cartridges expended for very few pigeons. One or two came late to ivy-covered tree. Birds like this sort of warm cover in which to tuck themselves up on cold nights. One or two were 'sitters'. Surprisingly easy to miss these. The motto is to use the choke barrel and shoot at the feet. When it was nearly dark, did exactly that at silhouette on oak branch. Unfortunately, it turned out to be a cock pheasant that had gone up to roost. The bird 'towered' nearly vertically and, squawking with justifiable outrage so that anyone for miles around could see and hear the nature of my offence, crashed—stone dead at my feet. Much chastened, I stuck it in the boot of the car. Consoled myself that keepers always have too many cocks over at the end of the season. Didn't mention it to Jack H, not that I think he or Mr Wallace would have been greatly concerned. Still, it did seem a breach of hospitality, even if unintentional. No excuse. Must be certain in future.

February 10th, 1964. Invited to shoot roosting wood near Chobham, Surrey. Snow again, starting to fall at midday. Decided to set out an hour early as snow looked as though it might really set in, in which case birds would come in early. In position at two-thirty, at least an hour earlier than usual. Snow only lightly powdered on floor of woods, so still possible to spot feathers and droppings under favoured roosting trees on edge of wood. By 3 pm a bitter wind had sprung up blowing outwards from wood so that any birds coming in would have to head it. Pigeons started almost at once. This was one of those 'pink bolster' days when you could see their blush-pink crops, stuffed with green food, bulging under their 'chins' as they approached the wood. These birds plainly sensed they were in for a long, bitter night and had packed their crops full of food. (It turned out later to be a mixture of kale and clover, so obviously they had switched from the more nourishing clover once the snow began to hide it.) They would get through the night digesting their crop contents.

Started shooting at once. Wind made some shots easy but about a third of the pigeons came in high, nearly closed their wings and slid down the wind like jet fighters. Did well to get one in three of these. By 4 pm snow had become a blizzard, but pigeons still piling in, some put out of trees by shooting and circling round over the tree tops completely disoriented. Simon, younger son armed with twenty-bore, got his share but was mainly occupied picking up with Drake, my big springer spaniel. Simon made piles of slain under prominent trees but soon these were covered by mounds of snow. Fitful moon behind snow clouds allowed shooting later than usual, but birds eventually tapered off. Even Drake had trouble finding piles of snow-covered birds. Believe we only lost half a dozen. Picked seventy-six. That was some roosting flight.

> NOTE: *If he can find a favoured roosting wood—fresh droppings and feathers are the sure indication—and pick the right night (a rough windy one) a roosting gun can make a fair impression on the local pigeon population. For the lone specialist who knows what he's doing, roosting takes some beating. No front cover is usually necessary. Background is vital. The secret of successful roost shooting is to shoot as if the twigs and branches aren't there. Enough of the pattern usually penetrates.*

March

March 1st, 5th, 10th, 1993. Oilseed rape, Clandon, Surrey. This crop is on a big estate which I 'look after' for pigeons with one other experienced pigeon gun. Apart from the pleasure of shooting regularly (as much as three or four days a week in the harvest) I feel it is a duty call whenever crops there are taking a bashing. This winter rape had really had it. For thirty or more yards into the field, it looked as though it had been worked on by a crazy army of ticket inspectors using old-fashioned ticket punches. Perhaps five hundred birds on a fifty-acre field. Net hide in hedge, but in different position on each of the three days to suit the wind.

Birds fairly easy to decoy on first day, thanks to stiffish breeze. First ten came in nicely but subsequent birds mainly overflew the decoys, though close enough to give a shot. Shot twenty-five before they decided they had had enough and moved to another rape field(?), anyway somewhere off the estate.

Shooting got progressively more difficult over the other two days. Total amounted to seventy-two birds all told, a number that won't make any difference in terms of damage but certainly had the effect of shifting the flock off a vulnerable and injured crop. The rape will probably recover. One result of such damage, I understand, is that eventual recovery results in 'secondary growth' which makes combining later on harder and less efficient.

NOTE: *Rape has now replaced clover as the pigeon's great winter and early spring standby. It can be extraordinarily difficult to shoot during March, as the birds are in large flocks and easily put off the field* en masse, *often never to return. Soon, the flocks will begin to break up for early breeding and will be feeding in the woods. Not, perhaps, the average pigeon shooter's favourite month!*

April

April 30th, 1970. Chawton Forest, Hants. Difficult few weeks of the pigeon year. Unexpectedly, found one part of our Forestry Commission shoot near Alton in Hampshire which the pigeons appeared to like. Found this by accident when doing some vermin shooting in preparation for the rearing season. Must get rid of some of the numerous magpies and jays if our few wild pheasants are to have a chance. Pigeons consistently using a flight-line off the field into a stand of tall beeches. Can only assume the beech buds were more to their liking than what they were finding outside. Nice wind and birds topping the big trees at the edge of the wood, just in range, rather like good driven pheasants only swinging about more. Had some decoys in the vehicle and a couple of hours to spare, so set out two dozen deeks on bare earth field outside the wood at what seemed to be the centre of the flight-line. Didn't expect the pigeons to come in to the decoys—though two actually did (got one). However, the decoys certainly chanelled them and made one or two dip to have a look. Didn't need a hide. Stood behind the root of a fallen silver birch. Great shooting. Very difficult. Got a dozen and was well pleased! Felt a bit guilty I hadn't put in more time with the magpies.

NOTE:*This is sometimes known as 'advanced decoying', in other words using decoys in an unusual situation to try to persuade birds to come within gun range. Doesn't always work. Worth trying. This time it paid off.*

May

May, almost any day, 1964. May can be the pigeon shooter's saddest month, though October can easily match it. The early paired birds are displaying and even nesting. Though feeding situations can still be found, most of the birds have returned to being true wood pigeons. Many are spending their days in the treetops, living off buds and florets. This is when that powerful, tearing beak, lacking in the other British wild pigeons and doves, comes into its own. When they're in the treetops, there is little the pigeon shooter can do about it.

At this period and for perhaps five years either side of 1964, I was exceedingly fortunate. So, in those days was the shooter who could decoy on the weed, charlock. Spraying has, to a large extent, exterminated that pigeon delicacy. But there is another weed on which the birds go quite dotty and in the years in question I was lucky to have access to a limitless supply of it. I am talking about chickweed. Happy is the pigeon shooter who knows a farmer who for one reason or another spares the chickweed. In those days, for one shilling a year, I had the shooting over some two hundred acres of nursery farm in outer suburbia which grew vegetables, good vegetables at that, for Covent Garden. It also, between the rows of lettuces, grew chickweed. This was neither sprayed nor mechanically eradicated and the woodies and stock doves (the latter then legitimate quarry) knew and appreciated the fact.

The farm was exactly five minutes from my house. It was not necessary to take nets or hide stakes. The vegetable rows were always stacked with the slatted wooden boxes in which the produce went to market. Eleven of these, and one to sit on, made the perfect hide. You could see through the gaps in the slats without being seen. Most important, the birds were used to seeing piles of boxes all around. Though the area was comparatively built-up, there were plenty of birds to give fifteen or twenty bags every time you went out. Some of the happiest hours I have spent were passed in those box castles with the mainline steam trains to Waterloo thundering past half a mile away and the smell of crushed mayweed strong and bitter in the nostrils.

NOTE: *I don't know quite what the moral of this story is unless it is that pigeon shooting can be found in the least expected places, even today, if you know what to look for and speak to the farmer nicely. Of course, not all May shooting depends on weeds. If you are lucky, you may find some young kale or mustard, and there may even be some peas still being drilled, though these days they roll them in deep and sometimes treat them with something that pigeons find unpalatable. There are more ways to protect a crop than by shooting.*

June

June 15th, 1968. Drove to Berkshire. Information from farmer this time correct. Too often a field reported 'blue with pigeons' has nothing on it when you get there. This was obviously 'it', a huge field of pig clover, that had been eaten down by pigeon during the winter and was well recovered. Enjoyed the supreme luxury of a bale hide. There is really no excuse for shooting badly from a bale hide. Sixteen bales are set up to form a hollow square in the centre of which the shooter sits on the seventeenth. The straw wall behind the shooter needs to be one bale taller than the rest to provide 'background' into which the shooter's head will disappear to an approaching pigeon.

The birds tried to come in even as I was setting out the decoys. Some difficulty in making the birds visible in the clover, but eventually found enough bare or flattened spaces. Decoys set to channel birds across the front of the hide heading into what wind there was. Feared the worst after few birds showed up once the first arrivals had taken fright. Waited an hour, remembering the Coats dictum: 'If they don't come back in twenty minutes, there is usually something wrong.' No real action until three in the afternoon. Then, as if a switch had been thrown, pigeons started to pile in, sometimes in parties of five or six. It should be easy enough to take a right and left out of these. In fact, it requires intense concentration and early decision as to which two you intend to kill. The first shot, of course, upsets the best-laid plans, pigeons being so agile in flight. Towards the end of the shoot, around 6 pm, I wasn't even bothering to set up dead birds, just leaving them as they fell, many belly up. The incomers weren't in the least put off. I had eighty when I picked up, with perhaps ten more lost. You can't really hunt the dogs on a shooting estate for lost birds when they fall in shelter belts and hedges where partridges and pheasants may be nesting.

NOTE: *This is just the sort of shoot that is difficult to find these days. Few 'modern' pigeons would be so obsessed with clover that they would ignore twenty or more of their slain colleagues lying on their backs with their feet in the air. We have taught them to be suspicious of even the most immaculate decoy set-up.*

July

July 10th, 1992. Clandon, Surrey. Amazing place this! Until the end of June there might not be a pigeon in Surrey. Then, suddenly, as the harvest ripens, the skies are full of them (at least in a good pigeon year). Shooting three and sometimes four days a week, bags are seldom below twenty or thirty and occasionally around the 'ton'. This day I'm in a hedge beneath a large ash, a known 'sitty tree', with decoys out on long narrow-laid patch of barley. When this set-up works, it is a classic one. The hedge channels birds directly from their home woods. The field is 'crowned', that is to say it rises up towards the middle so that the far hedge is in dead ground from my hide. However, there are two solitary oaks close to the 'crown'. Birds approaching from other directions sit in these, see the decoys or, more likely, see birds coming in to them and fly across the field to take a look. The shooter thus has two lines of approach and a third if you include birds sitting in the ash who decide to decoy. Of course, it doesn't always turn out that way. This day, despite the fact there was little wind, it did. Birds decoyed from all three directions. Ran out of cartridges at 3 pm and had to walk back to the Land Rover for my reserve supply. Picked 152 before the pigeons had had enough around five in the afternoon. I daresay if I had stuck it out they would have started again later.

July 30th, 1993. Kingsclere, Hants. Birds on large wheat field but refused to decoy. Noticed flight-line to hedge close to pig farm buildings. Steady trickle of birds travelling that way, landing and, after a minute or two, taking off again. Guessed correctly, for once, that the attraction was a water trough. Birds on grain, especially wheat, it seems, develop a tremendous thirst. Set up nets in hedge on flight-line to trough and put two decoys on fence posts beside trough itself. Shot twenty-two before pigeons tired of the game and went to look for a drink somewhere else.

NOTE: *Pigeons usually start the harvest festival on wheat and then switch to barley. I have had most of my big bags on this estate on barley, though once the harvest ripens generally, they can be fickle and dine where they find the menu most to their liking. There's usually a preferred field and even a preferred patch. As always, there is no substitute for watching and waiting. Luckily, with net hides, a move can be made very quickly.*

August

August 18th, 1993. Clandon. Hooray for oilseed rape. If only there wasn't so much of it! Pigeons, however, appear to find an oilseed rape stubble irresistible. How they spot the small brown seeds left by the combine beats me. Once they have adjusted their 'search image', however, they obviously have no difficulty. Decoys show up well. Apart from the tall, stiff stubble spikes of the rape plants, the earth is bare. Set up in nets under lone oak. Birds channelled beautifully round it and into decoy pattern. Shot forty-seven before they decided another rape stubble might be healthier. Next day, however, these or other birds were back. From the same position I shot another thirty-seven. This went on with slight changes of position for over a week. Then the tractor appeared to start turning the stubble in. Birds decoyed even while the tractor was turning at the other end of the field.

NOTE: *There is only one snag to rape stubble. Once it rains hard, the seeds germinate and produce small green rape plants in which the pigeons aren't the least bit interested while there is a grain or another rape stubble available.*

September

September 2nd, 1989. Kingsclere, Hants. Barley stubble with hide on edge of wood. Birds from wood seeing decoys (nearly fifty yards out from trees) and turning back and in to decoys. Shoot helped by strong wind. A situation in which realism counts. Fortunately, had a dozen dead birds from deep-freeze to start with and then set out shot birds with twig under beak to support head in lifelike attitude. Have no doubt that without this attention to detail, and nearly gale-force wind, birds might have gone somewhere else. An interesting exercise in what Archie might have called 'advanced decoying'. Shot twenty-two and felt lucky to have done so well.

NOTE: *Stubbles remain one of the main sources of food once the harvest is over. These days, sadly for the pigeon shooter and therefore the pigeon, intensive farming gets tractor, harrow and plough on to the barley and wheat fields almost as soon as they are combined. If you can find a promising stubble, one perhaps that is to become set-aside or is undersown with clover, you may get some excellent shooting. These days, pigeons don't depend on stubble grain nearly so much. Winter rape soon comes in to fill the gap.*

October

October, 1970. Micheldever, Hants. A good acorn and beech mast year. Pigeons feeding in the woods so very difficult to get at, unless a regular flight-line can be found. In this case, birds were consistently flighting to a small isolated stand of beech. Taking them as they came over the edge of the wood.

Decoys set out on bare plough in attempt to 'pull' the flight-line. Doubt if they made much difference. Birds very high due to lack of wind but offering magnificent overhead shots. Shot eleven for thirty-three cartridges and felt quite pleased. At least as difficult as tall pheasants and a lot more aerobatic. Reckon those eleven birds were worth three times the number shot over decoys.

NOTE: *Often the low point of the pigeon shooter's year. Beech mast and acorns give the birds a better return for time spent searching and nutriment gained than even a generously stocked wheat or barley stubble.*

November

November 10th, 1978. Selsey, Sussex. I put this one in as a one-off and as a further example of opportunism and flight-line shooting. The two are often synonymous. While doing some work on our shoot at Selsey in a gale-force wind I noticed some pigeons coming steadily into the wind from the direction of Sidlesham and out towards the sea wall. Between Ham Farm and the wall, and off our boundary, are some rough grazing meadows. Without being able to examine the meadows, I would guess that they were well stocked with clover and that this was the attraction. Pigeons know almost as much about using the wind as albatrosses. By flying six to ten feet off the deck they were using a layer of air where the wind force was reduced by friction with the ground. As often demonstrated by strong-flying birds who know where they are going, they seemed to be boring into the wind with undiminished speed. No hide was needed, just a willingness to jump down into the bottom of a water-filled ditch. After a few adjustments of position, I managed to get into the centre of the traffic. No decoys needed. In forty-five minutes I had shot ten and missed as many more. My companion got a further six and declared it to have been far more exciting than driven pheasants.

NOTE: *Flight-line shooting can be not only exciting but also extremely productive. Two friends of mine earlier in the year in which I write shot in a day over six hundred birds flighting over their own land to feed in a field on which they did not have permission to shoot!*

December

December 10th, 1976. Sutton Scotney, Hants. Pig clover being heavily set upon. Shot from bale hide, starting at nine in the morning and ending at three in the afternoon. This was a similar field and crop to one on which Archie Coats shot his record bag. My efforts (and that of the pigeons, incidentally) on this occasion were nothing like as productive as the Master's. However, I got forty-five but should have had at least sixty.

NOTE: *On the day described, I started shooting at nine in the morning, which may have been an hour late. In winter, pigeons feed early and get as much in as they can before the short daylight fails them. One further observation. Sutton Scotney was then one of the great sporting estates in Hampshire, if not the greatest. Despite this, head keepers and beat keepers, provided you play ball with them, keep them fully informed and get their permission to shoot, are not usually concerned about the noise of pigeon shooting disturbing game. Obviously, you must keep clear of main coverts and make sure that no shoots are planned in the near future for that part of the estate. All through the year, whether in nets or bale hides, in many different situations and locations, I have watched game birds parade within ten yards of my position without showing the slightest concern.*

This brief 'almanac' does, I hope, indicate that pigeon shooting can be found the year round, provided one plays fair with farmers and keepers. That said, pigeon shooting is not as easy to find as it was fifteen or even ten years ago. These days many farmers sell pigeon shooting for around £25 per day, sometimes more.

9

The Wood Pigeon, Any Answers?

WHERE the wood pigeon, its population, its future, its control is concerned, there are plenty of questions. There are also at this moment plenty of experts seeking the answers. BASC has set up its Wood Pigeon Working Party whose main task is to study the effect and the effectiveness of shooting as a means of protecting the farmer and, of course, providing continued sport. The NFU, in association with BASC, aims to survey the farmers' view of shooting as a means of crop protection. The Ministry of Agriculture, and particularly its Pest Infestation Department, continues its studies of wood pigeon behaviour and biology at Carlton in Cambridgeshire. The British Trust for Ornithology is working with the Joint Nature Conservation Committee to devise a method of estimating the true pigeon population of Great Britain. Because of the ubiquity and density of the bird, this has hitherto proved a daunting task. The Game Conservancy is undertaking a study of ringing recoveries throughout Europe over the last few decades, not only of the wood pigeon but of the other dove species.

All this adds up to a great deal of research, research which cannot possibly produce any answers for at least five years. Though later editions of this book may be able to include the results, I can only give some preliminary findings and, let's admit it, 'guestimates'. Some of them are my own, but my betting is that when all the analysts have done their homework and the computers have stopped clicking and flashing, some of these informed guesses won't be so far from the truth.

As I said in the introduction, these research programmes have suddenly become necessary and urgent because of the EU's proposal—temporarily postponed as far as Britain is concerned—that all its member countries should impose a long close season for the wood pigeon. To British farmers and sportsmen who daily witness great flocks of wood pigeon feeding on farm produce, this seemed a lunatic proposal. How on earth, they asked, did it ever come about?

The answer, I believe, is to be found some years back in Germany when the activities of their Green Party were at their height. From Germany the demand to protect *Columba palumbus* spread to France and then to the bureaucrats in Brussels. The Green Party's cry was that the wood pigeon was a migratory bird, and like many migratory birds, persecuted by the several countries through which it passed.

The lobbyists were perfectly correct in one respect. In Europe the wood pigeon *is* a migratory bird. Whenever I travel through France, I am amazed at the small numbers of wood pigeon I see in apparently favourable rural areas. But my journeys are usually made in summer. Were I in the south and in particular in the Pyrenees in late September and October the impression might be a very different one.

This is the time when *le pigeon ramier* pours south through the passes, sometimes crossing the mountains at heights of five thousand feet or more. This is also the time of *les colombières*, the pigeon catchers on both sides of the frontier who use traditional methods going back many hundred years. Their techniques and equipment include wooden paddles, painted grey and white, which are thrown into the air as the pigeon flocks fly through the passes. The falling paddles (an effect similar to that used by the decoy shooter when throwing a dead bird out of the hide) make the flocks fly lower. Further up the pass are relays of other paddle throwers who eventually bring the pigeons low enough to fly into a net.

Different villages use different methods: spring nets released by a watcher in a hut when the migrants have been decoyed onto a feed; lines of hides across the top of a *col* for shooters; mysterious contraptions for hoisting rows of decoys up trees; look-out posts on tall pylons. The fact that many of these traditional methods involve the use of live pigeon decoys, some of the birds hooded, no doubt incensed the protectionists further. It is unlikely that the entire annual bag of the *colombières* both on the French and Spanish sides of the Pyrenees approaches that of half a dozen serious decoy shooters in Great Britain, but there is little doubt that it was this harvesting of the southward migration of European wood pigeons that led the EU Commissioners to turn their attention to Britain.

Not all European wood pigeons migrate, of course, but there is no doubt that the majority do so. The main routes are through the Pyrenees, many birds heading for the acorns of the cork oak forests of Spain. Others turn towards the Atlantic coast of Brittany. Another stream passes through the Swiss Alps to Italy. Some of the birds from western Russia,

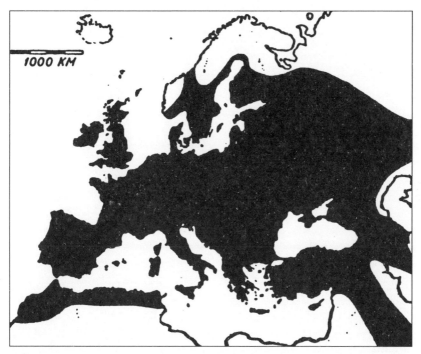

World distribution of wood pigeon and sub-species.
Sub-species also occur in the Canary Islands and Maderia.

Poland and Denmark swing south-west through the Pyrenees, but a high proportion of the Russian pigeons and those of the north German plain stay put, only moving south in really hard weather.

It is easier to understand the call for a close season—most European countries already have one—when you know the comparatively small wood pigeon populations of our main European partners. France has an estimated two million birds; Germany, two million; Holland, one million; Sweden, one million six hundred thousand; Finland, three hundred and thirty thousand. Compare this with Great Britain with at least fifteen million birds.

The argument that Britain eventually put successfully to the EU was that the migration problem did not affect the British Isles since our huge wood pigeon population never leaves home. Why should it? As has been previously pointed out, wood pigeons do not care for flying over large stretches of water. They like to see trees and fields below them rather than waves. Moreover, the temperate climate of these islands suits them very well. Hardship only comes to them in exceptional winters such as that of 1962-3. Even when cold weather strikes, they seem to have lost the urge or instinct to leave the country. Finally, British agriculture and forestry provide them with everything they need for a full, rich and successful life.

As to migration *into* Britain. Though many countrymen, and not a few pigeon shooters, still maintain that there is an autumn movement into Britain by Scandinavian birds—the usual story is that they are smaller and darker—there is absolutely no evidence for this. Murton's researches (and not only aboard the ill-fated Goodwin Sands lightship) effectively proved that. There *is* often an internal movement of wood pigeons in Britain, flocks moving into new areas in late autumn, but these birds haven't come from overseas, even though some may appear to have done so. For example, some flocks may have taken a short cut across part of the Wash, and thus appear to the watcher on the shore to have crossed the North Sea. Moreover, the 'darker, smaller' birds are almost certainly juveniles, young of the past breeding season.

By skilfully presenting these arguments, British farming, sporting and environmental interests were able to persuade the European Commissioners that there was no case in the UK for a close season. However, it cannot be said too often that the threat has not entirely gone away. In the words of Dr John Harradine, BASC's Research Director, 'the Department of the Environment is required to monitor the population so that it does not become an endangered species.'

The Game Conservancy's part in the current research work is tied closely to the movement of pigeons both in the UK and throughout Europe. To date, 65,000 pigeons and doves have been ringed in Great Britain of which 3,600 rings have been recovered, many by shooters. The recovery of ringed birds in Europe is, naturally, much higher. Recoveries of rings there to date total 5,600. Finland alone has ringed 2,037 pigeons since 1972 of which 224 have been recovered, mostly in France, though one bird reached Corsica. Amazingly, one Finnish wood pigeon was found to be thirteen years old. (What is the average age in the wild? Almost certainly only three or four years.)

To the layman such as myself, even 5,600 recoveries seems a remarkably small sample from which to draw conclusions. Nicholas Aebischer, Head of Biometrics at the Game Conservancy, assures me that this is not the case:

> The Game Conservancy is interested in the pan-European view of the impact of shooting on the pigeon family in general, not only the wood pigeon, but stock doves, collared doves and even turtle doves. We shall carry out a comparative analysis of ringing recoveries for all four species throughout the whole of Europe. From this we should be able to calculate the survival rates for the four species going back twenty years. It should also reveal the importance of shooting in controlling population compared with other factors such as weather, agricultural and legislative changes and so on.

The impact of shooting is something that concerns everyone involved in this research programme. Indeed, it is the main theme in the investigations of scientists, sportsmen and farmers alike, though each approaches the question from a slightly different direction. The basic questions are: how many wood pigeons are shot each year? And what effect does shooting have on the total population? As long ago as 1953 to 1960, during the government-subsidised shooting scheme, the official bag returns were over two million birds per annum, although it is quite possible that returns were exaggerated to justify the issue of yet more subsidised cartridges. Murton's estimate was that of a probable total of ten million birds, five million could be killed without affecting the size of the wood pigeon population. The

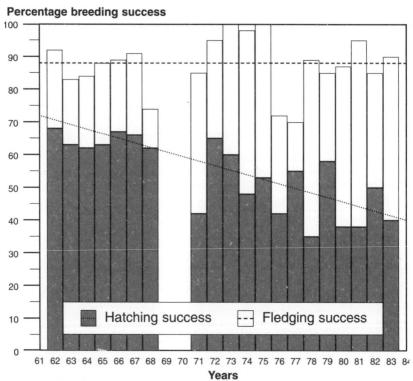

Percentage breeding success

Years

Hatching success means percentage of eggs hatched; fledging success, percentage of hatched eggs that produced fledged young.

survival rate per nesting pair then was 2.8. In the 1960s of all eggs laid sixty-five per cent hatched. Today this is down to thirty-five per cent. Interestingly enough, the survival rate of young to flying stage from those eggs that do hatch remains constant at eighty-five per cent.

John Harradine's calculations, made as the result of the National Shooting Survey held in 1980 and 1987, suggest that the total annual bag made by BASC members lay somewhere between two million and 4.4 million wood pigeons. But this did not take into account those shot by non-members who probably outnumber BASC members by three to one. However, for whatever reason, maybe simply because they were keener or better at it, BASC guns shot twice as many as non-BASC guns. At this point, John Harradine makes a guestimate himself saying: 'this suggests that the total British bag of wood pigeons could lie between four and eight million birds.' He sums it ups totally truthfully by saying: 'Whether or not this estimate is close to the true figure, it is clear that the total kill is not greater than the population can withstand since it is in a healthy and increasing state.'

BASC's current researches are aimed very much at getting a realistic bag figure. Though, as Harradine states, the population appears to be a healthy and increasing one, the survival rate of young per nesting pair has now fallen to around 1.6. Since the population is increasing, there has to be some other factor accounting for this success. The most likely explanation is the abundance of winter and early spring food, namely oilseed rape. But if the planting of this crop fell drastically, for whatever reason, it is possible that the wood pigeon would decline with it and that overshooting would then be a significant factor in the equation. For this reason alone, BASC's researches are of prime importance.

To date, there is no doubt that shooting has failed significantly to reduce Britain's wood pigeon population. Apart from the sport it provides for the shooter and the £1.3 million said to be derived from sales of pigeon meat, does shooting wood pigeons really benefit anyone and most of all the farming community?

Research by the scientists O'Connor and Shrubb even suggests that decoy shooting over crops could have a counter-productive effect. Their point is that the social structure and heirarchy within a flock may influence the feeding behaviour of its members. Shoot some of its members and you may create a vacuum into which other birds, presumably lower in the pecking order, may move, thereby maintaining the level of crop damage despite the shooting effort!

The simple decoy shooter cannot be expected to take such scientific niceties into consideration. To him, one fewer pigeon is one fewer to eat the crop, so load up and have a go at the next one. And you really can't blame him for that. Nor can you blame the scientists of the Ministry of Agriculture for trying to find cheaper or more effective ways of protecting the farmer. Are there cheaper or more effective ways?

Narcotics had their brief day in the 1960s but experiments showed they were no respecters of song and game birds and their use, except in expert hands, indescriminate and unreliable.

Reproductive inhibitors—birth control methods for wood pigeons—might be effective provided the difficulties of selective baiting could be overcome. As with narcotics, there would be ecological, emotional and political difficulties.

The planting of alternative food crops, as is practised in Holland to keep geese off vulnerable farmland, is largely a non-starter for pigeons, though some set-aside land might be used in this way. Some large bags, including the current record of 563 (see chapter 6) have been shot on set-aside. The trouble with wood pigeons is that they are ubiquitous. The bulk of the flock eventually finds some commercial crop it wants, even if some birds can be lured on to food grown specially for them.

Some damage, particularly to oilseed rape, might be limited if the farmer could be more selective about the fields in which he grows it. Pigeons like undisturbed fields, therefore the fields that are in sight of dwellings or barns in constant use are, in theory, less likely to be attacked, though my own experience is that pigeons soon become used to harmless human traffic such as tractors. What might be called topographical defence would include putting your peas or young rape half a mile from the principle roosting wood and close to a main road. Such measures, however, are not realistic and are unlikely to fit into any farmer's programme of crop rotation. There is, however, an increase in the planting of spring as opposed to winter oilseed rape—for economic reasons, rather than to reduce pigeon damage in winter. Nevertheless, it tends to have that effect.

Siting of new woods as a result of woodland farming schemes can effect the number of pigeons in the area. Pigeons, as has been shown, like to nest on the outskirts of woods rather than at their centre. If woodland is to be increased, it has been suggested that consideration should be given to adding to existing woods, rather than planting a number of new small copses. Pigeons usually nest within twenty yards of the outside of a wood. Small woods therefore suit their reproductive purposes best. However, farmers and landowners have very strong views about where they want their woodland. Woods are usually sited for very good reasons such as providing shelter or game cover and not for discouraging nesting pigeons!

Audio defences? The rural public does not greatly appreciate having its calm shattered by a barrage of gas guns. Such guns do, undoubtedly, have a deterrent effect (witness the number of pigeon shooters who obtain the farmer's permission to turn the bangers off when they are decoying in the same or a nearby field). However, a lot depends on the timing of the gas gun's use. Bring it into action too early and the birds may become habituated to it. The farmer needs his artillery at a time when his crop is at its maximum vulnerability. Guns that fire an irregular pattern of 'shots' rather than those that go bang at precisely the same interval have something to commend them.

That there is a limit to the public's tolerance of noise defence of crops was demonstrated by a story in *The Times* of July, 1994. A Somerset farmer was ordered by the environmental health officials of Taunton Deane to switch off an amplified tape recording that included the sounds of street riots, elephants trumpeting and Bob Geldof singing. This machine, the 'Pest-Off', developed by Martley Electronics, was intended to keep the pigeons off Mr Vaughan's two hundred acres of rape. The reaction of the neighbours is well documented; that of the pigeons not recorded.

Scarecrows are as old as agriculture. Where pigeons are concerned, such variants as 'flash harries' (brightly-coloured moving objects), cut out figures of men with guns, fertiliser bags suspended on poles all have a limited use. The correct time to put out such bird-scarers is at the start of the danger period and before the flocks form a feeding habit on that particular field. In time, though, pigeons get used to all these deterrents, especially if the weather has sharpened their hunger and there is no other equally nourishing food source within range.

Dr Ian Inglis carried out some interesting experiments using pigeon wings as potential pigeon scarers at Carlton. Murton had suggested as long ago as 1974 that pigeons preferred not to settle among decoys with open wings. The wood pigeon has no alarm call, so a visual signal or signals might well do the job for it instead. If, as previous shooting experiments at Carlton had tended to show, pigeons were put off by open-winged decoys, then it seemed likely that the visible signals that deterred them were the bird's white wing bars. The fact that these white marks are also thought to be a food attraction signal, given by a bird landing on a crop to birds already in the air, did not necessarily detract from the possibility. Aversive, or turn-off, signals are often closely allied to attractive ones. Exaggerate the attractive stimuli and you frequently achieve the opposite effect.

Accordingly, Inglis produced some pigeon wings with various wing-bar modifications, including some without wing-bars, some with double wing-bars and others with the wing-bar greatly increased in width by the use of white paint. The double-width bars proved the greatest deterrent. Moreover, the experiments showed that it was not necessary to put out whole birds as decoys. Just the wings mounted on wire frames would do as well.

Field trials lasting several months confirmed that these modified wings, used in sufficient quantity did give a significant measure of crop protection.

In an allied piece of research, Inglis examined the deterrent effect of those same white wing markings oscillating at the speed of a wood pigeon's wings when taking off in alarm. Plainly, a bird taking off in a panic would be likely to leave the scene with a wing-beat faster than normal. Inglis found it was possible to reproduce different speeds of wing-bar oscillation by means of a white-painted rotating vane. In trials these devices were found to be more effective than commercial visual scarers, such as 'flash harries'. Inglis sadly concluded that it was unlikely that any commercial firm would see an opportunity in marketing rotating wing-bar oscillators. Nor are farmers likely to take the trouble to decorate their crops with a number of inevitably fragile double-width wing-bar pigeon wings on wire frames!

Nest-poking remains another possible method of trying to control wood pigeon numbers. Until the 1970s, nest-pokers were employed during the breeding season by Rabbit Clearance Societies who were then partly subsidised by the Ministry of Agriculture. The success of this approach depended upon the knowledge and conscientiousness of the individuals doing the job. According to the Ministry's Advisory Leaflet No. 165, two men could poke eighty acres of nesting woodland twice in the vital period when pigeons had eggs or young in the nest. The pokers took 320 man-hours to do so. At the time, it cost one shilling and sixpence to poke a nest. Destroying nests by means of long poles from the ground was not found to be cost-effective then, and there is little likelihood that it would be found any cheaper or more cost-effective now.

There seems no doubt at all that, as Murton showed, that it is food supply that controls pigeon numbers, and winter and early spring food supply most of all. The advent of oilseed rape gave the wood pigeon a tremendous boost. The acreage of oilseed rape rose steadily until 1991. Since then it has begun to fall. To a very large extent, the bird's success depends on the current pattern of farming, which in turn depends on many factors, not least on EU subsidies. When considering the future of the wood pigeon population in Britain, this is where the great imponderables lie. An alteration in farming policy here or in Brussels could sway the balance greatly in either direction. No one would be rash enough to forecast which. What can be said with total certainty—and you don't need to be a scientist to say it—is that *Columba palumbus* is one of the most successful vacuum-fillers in all nature. Give it a niche and it will fill it to the maximum capacity.

It is clear that shooting, at least in the bird's present state of abundance, can never make serious inroads into Britain's wood pigeon hordes. I have declared my interest as a regular wood-pigeon shooter, so you must make what allowance you wish for my personal bias. However, I have no doubt at all that shooting over endangered crops can restrict damage and may in some circumstances even save a complete crop from destruction.

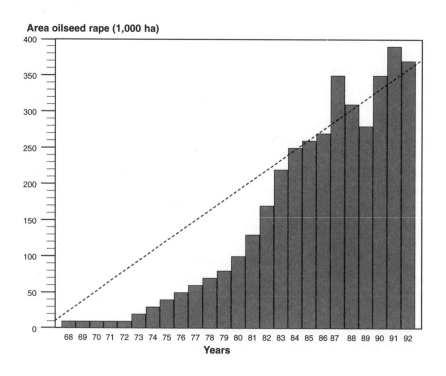

Mean numbers of fledged young per pair

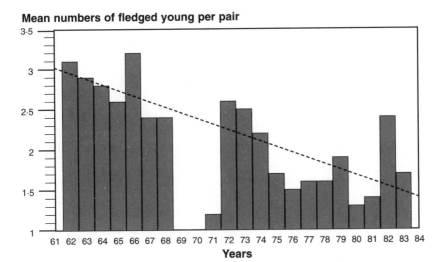

Indeed, shooting may have far more than a local effect. The survival rate per pair has fallen from 2.8 young in Ron Murton's day to around 1.6 per pair at the moment. A probable reason for this is increased predation by corvids, notably jays and magpies. Shooting during the nesting season reduces the level of parental care, simply because some adult wood pigeons with young at nest get shot. In normal circumstances, both male and female care for their young in their early stages. One stays at the nest, while the other goes off to feed. If one parent has fallen to a decoy shooter, then the nest must, perforce, be left unguarded when the surviving adult goes to feed. Jays and magpies patrol nesting sites regularly. An unguarded nest with two white eggs in it is a sitting target for the sharp-eyed corvid. Gamekeepers, most of whom these days rear tame birds, have no time and little need to destroy magpies and jays in the spring. They are fully occupied in their rearing sheds and fields. So magpies and jays multiply. Their nest-robbing activities are certainly one reason why the production of young pigeons has fallen so dramatically, though, of course, there may be other contributory factors, including egg predation by rats and even in some areas, by blackheaded gulls.

Per cent eggs predated

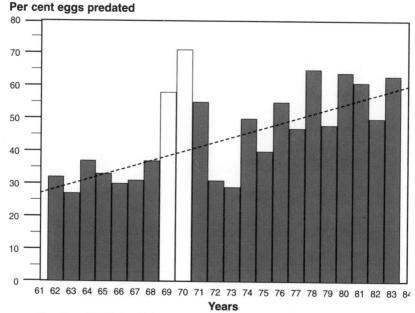

Years

Open bars (69, 70) show high predation rates when numbers of pigeon were shot during the nesting period and nests left unguarded by parents.

Where magpies and jays are concerned, the modern keeper has a powerful ally in the fully-approved Larsen trap which catches corvids for him while he is engaged on rearing tasks. The Larsen trap, which lures magpies and crows by use of a live decoy, may help to tip the balance in the nesting wood pigeon's favour.

There are a few pluses in the economy of the wood pigeon. Whereas, not so long ago, farmers welcomed responsible pigeon shooters on to their land to protect crops, the practice of charging pigeon shooters for their sport is on the increase and will almost certainly grow, as farmers' profit margins shrink. European guns, German, Dutch and Italian, in particular, are coming over in growing numbers to shoot British pigeons, and very good some of them are at it. Britain has the birds. British farmers have a pigeon problem. Most European countries have a long close season for wood pigeons. So foreign guns are more than happy to be taken out by expert guides and to spend quite large sums in Britain for their sport. There are, therefore, several good economic reasons, apart from the purely sporting or agricultural ones, for backing pigeon shooting.

The export trade in pigeons is probably worth well over £1.5 million. In Europe, in France most of all, *le pigeon ramier* is regarded as a gourmet dish for which excellent money is paid. Alas, the same cannot be said of the British housewife. Several reasons why she should change her opinion are given in the concluding chapter of this book.

10

The Wood Pigeon in the Kitchen

WOOD pigeon is extremely healthy fare. Like venison, it has little or no fat on it. No one should be surprised that pigeons taste as good as they do, seeing that they spend their entire lives feeding on the very best vegetable produce the countryside can provide.

Yet, one of several canards about the wood pigeon is that it is indigestible. I have even come across an old wives' tale which says that you would die if you ate a pigeon a day for a month, though of what I cannot begin to guess. I have never tried an unrelenting thirty-day diet of wood pigeon, although I would be quite willing to do so in the interests of medical science. Pigeon in one form or another is certainly delicious enough to eat for a month on end. However, most people prefer to vary their diet. I hazard that you would not wish to eat caviare every day for a month, although I am still waiting for someone to ask me. The pigeon fable, like most fables, does not merit close examination. Unlike many fables, it does not contain even the faintest element of truth. But, strange though it may seem, you may find some guests who prefer not to be told they have eaten pigeon.

Prue Coats, cookery expert wife of the late Archie Coats, has written several first-class cookery books packed with wonderful pigeon recipes, two of which I include here. If Prue does not know how to cook the delectable bird, then no one on earth does. In her long culinary career she has had to overcome what she calls 'the pigeon pie mentality'. What she means by this is that most people assume that the only thing you can do with wood pigeon is to casserole it for ever or stick it in a pie. Well, you *can* do both those things, but they overlook the superb virtuosity of the wood pigeon in the kitchen of an imaginative and skilful cook.

As to casseroling the bird 'for ever', the basic truth about pigeon which few people realise is this. You have two alternatives – sauté the breast meat for a maximum of three minutes a side (if cut in strips, often as little as one minute) or cook it slow and long *en casserole*. Believe me, incredible as it seems, there is nothing in between these two alternatives.

The following recipes offer a range of gourmet dishes within these two fundamental approaches to pigeon cuisine.

Pigeon Stroganoff

Serves 4

Among the friends whose illusions were not shattered on being told the substance of the delicacy they had just eaten with such obvious delight, were two to whom we served Pigeon Stroganoff, my wife Joan's invention, or rather adaptation. This is made exactly the same way as the classic dish invented by Mr Stroganoff, except that you use thinly-sliced slivers of pigeon breast instead of thinly sliced slivers of expensive rump steak. Two breasts or one pigeon per person is about right.

8 pigeon breasts
6 oz/175 g butter
8 oz/225 g button mushrooms
1 onion, sliced
½ pint sour cream
freshly-ground salt and pepper

Cookery books suggest that you should sauté your beef before immersing it in the sauce for 5 to 7 minutes. Try that with pigeon and you will end up with something very like fried biltong. One minute a side in very hot butter is all that is needed. It is pretty hard to judge which side you have done when the pan is filled with slivers of meat, so I suggest you just turn the pigeon breasts in 4 oz/110 g butter, stir-frying, until the outside of the meat is sealed and brown and the inside is still pink and tender. I usually nick a bit out of the pan and test it to see if the strips of meat are done.

In another pan, cook the onion and sliced mushrooms in the rest of the butter. Season and add to the sautéed pigeon. Add the sour cream, preferably warmed, and check the seasoning.

As an accompaniment, mashed creamed potatoes are good, but plain boiled rice is better.

In my opinion all these quick sautéed pigeon dishes should be eaten hot from the oven. This is a nuisance for the host or hostess who wants to be with the guests as much as possible. The solution is to own an electric 'hostess' which keeps the food hot without drying or cooking it. The pigeon will come to no harm if immersed in the sour cream and mushroom sauce. But, if you are cooking for yourself, take my advice and eat at once!

Minced Pigeon

When we have a surplus of pigeons, we mince up a number of pigeon breasts and my wife uses this minced pigeon meat in several ways. For instance, she makes traditional cottage or shepherd's pies. These can be stashed away in the deep freeze for those days when you come in tired and possibly wet or frozen and wonder what you can eat that is easy, nourishing, warming and doesn't come in a supermarket packet.

If you like pasta dishes, then minced pigeon does excellently in lasagne.

The raw mince can be frozen in bags and put away in the freezer until needed.

Stir-fry Pigeons

Serves 4

Pigeon does extremely well in a wok. Like many other cooks, I like to 'slurp' vino when cooking. It helps the process. When stir-frying pigeon, I usually tip some dry vermouth or sherry into the wok, as well.

8 pigeon breasts (2 per person)
soy sauce
olive oil
1 green, 1 red pepper, sliced thinly

1 broccoli head, broken into small pieces
8 oz/225 g mushrooms, sliced
2-4 tomatoes, sliced
1 or 2 sticks celery, chopped

I like to cook the vegetables first and the pigeon extremely quickly once the vegetables are out of the wok and in the oven or 'hostess'. So stir-fry the vegetables in olive oil and transfer them to a warm dish in a cool oven or 'hostess'. Cut the breasts into slim strips as for Stroganoff and sauté in olive oil (see previous remarks on sauté-ing slivers of pigeon breasts) and add to the vegetables. Wok dishes are best prepared individually, but are so quick to produce that this causes little delay at the table.

Pigeon with Paté or Liver Sausage

Another great Joan Willock invention which is easy to make. She says you don't need the bird 'in the round', that is with the breast still attached to the back, just the breast bone with meat in place. (See my notes on preparing pigeon for cooking later in this chapter.)

1 pigeon breast on the bone per person
6 or more rashers of streaky bacon
paté or liver sausage, about 2 oz/50 g per portion
1 tablespoon lemon juice
salt and pepper

Line the bottom of a roasting tin with streaky bacon. Pack the cavity of each breast with liver sausage or paté. Season with freshly ground salt and black pepper. Lay the birds, breast-side down to begin with, on the bacon. Cover with more streaky bacon and squirt some lemon juice over them. The lemon juice was a happy experiment the first time, which seemed to work well and has done ever since. Cook on a low heat, gas mark 4/350°F/180°C, until tender, about 1 hour. Turn the pieces of pigeon, half way through cooking time.

New potatoes and peas go very well with this dish.

Prue's Smoked Pigeon Paté

For this recipe you will need one of those hot-smokers you can buy in most fishing tackle or good kitchen shops. With all due respect to Prue Coats who invented this recipe, I play around with herbs and spices a bit to suit my own taste. Instead of the ground ginger and runny honey, I now substitute Messrs Culpepper's honey and ginger juice. Expensive but good, it should be kept in the fridge once uncorked.

8 pigeon breasts
5 rashers streaky bacon
3 oz/80 g finely-chopped onions or shallots
4 oz/110 g unsalted butter
4 fl oz/120 ml Vermouth
1 teaspoon runny honey
2 teaspoons lemon juice
1 teaspoon dried ground ginger
1 tablespoon double cream
¼ teaspoon ground cloves
1 teaspoon Dijon mustard
a pinch of dill weed
salt and ground pepper

To smoke the pigeon breasts, sprinkle one tablespoon of the sawdust supplied with the hot-smoker on the base of the smoker, place the pigeon breasts on the grid and cover with half the streaky bacon. You need the pan juices from the smoker later on, so I lay silver foil over the grid with the edges slightly turned up to hold the juice and prevent it leaking away. Slide the lid on the smoker and put it over the methylated spirit burners supplied with the kit, light and allow to burn out. This takes about 10 minutes.

Sauté the remaining bacon and the onion in butter until the onion is transparent but not brown, and then transfer to the food processor. Now dice the smoked pigeon breasts and sauté for a few seconds in the remaining butter stirring all the while. Pour juices from smoker into pan, plus all the other ingredients, including cream and seasonings. Stir and turn up the heat so the mixture bubbles. Let it bubble hard for a few seconds. Add to the food processor, process all until finely ground and then pour in the pan juices and blend until smooth. Put into small bowls or margarine containers. Leave in the fridge to amalgamate flavour for a day. This paté deep-freezes excellently. Decorate each container with a green bay leaf or two before freezing.

Pigeon Breasts Stuffed with Garlic Cheese

Another Prue Coats number, and quite delicious.

2 pigeon breasts per person
Rondele or Boursin or pepper Boursin cheese
2 egg yolks
2 oz/50 g freshly-made breadcrumbs
2 tablespoons seasoned flour

Slit each breast with a sharp knife to form a pocket in it. Fill this as full as possible with garlic cheese. (Prue suggests Rondele but Boursin is nearly as good and pepper Boursin possibly better.) Shake each breast in a bag filled with seasoned flour, and then egg and breadcrumb them. If necessary, give them a second treatment with breadcrumbs to ensure they are well covered. I often prepare a whole lot of these breasts and put them away in the deep-freeze until needed. For immediate use it is probably best to leave them in the fridge for a few hours. Sauté the breasts for 3–4 minutes a side. Serve immediately, although once again they can fairly safely be reserved in the electric 'hostess'.

Any that are over can be left to cool and then sliced thinly with a sharp knife. They make an excellent basis for a salad. We once served this as a starter to two nervous guests who might not have enjoyed it so much if they had known they were eating pigeon. After a lot of discussion, we decided to tell them it was stuffed venison. Since neither of our friends had ever plucked a pigeon or skinned a roe deer—or were ever likely to—we thought this innocent deception was quite safe. I was a bit stumped when asked how one managed to insert the cheese into the venison, and, by the way, what part of the deer did one use, but managed to talk my way out of it fairly convincingly—or so I thought.

Pigeon Escalopes with Honey and Ginger

Culpepper's Malaysian Ginger Juice with Honey makes a lovely accompaniment to sautéed pigeon breasts. This time, omit the cheese stuffing. Three minutes a side, no more, in foaming butter to which a tablespoon or two of Ginger Juice has been added. Reserve breasts when done, add some more Ginger Juice to the pan and caramelise it with butter and pan juices. Spoon this over the breasts as a sauce. Delicious.

Pigeon Pâté (from the Hungry Monk)

Serves 12

I have long been a fan of the recipes published by Hungry Monk Publications, an off-shoot of that marvellous restaurant, The Hungry Monk at Jevington, near Polegate, Sussex. I reproduce these next two gourmet recipes with their very kind permission.

6 pigeon breasts
6 oz/175 g minced pork
4 oz/110 g minced ox liver
4 oz/110 g minced chicken liver
4 oz/110 g streaky bacon
1 large onion
2 oz/50 g butter
1/4 pint/150 ml double cream
two tots brandy
2 glasses red wine
4 cloves garlic
freshly-ground salt and black pepper

Finely dice the pigeon breasts and the onion. Crush the garlic with a little salt. Pre-heat the oven to gas mark 1/275°F/140°C.

Melt the butter in a deep pan. Fry the onion until golden before adding the minced chicken liver, ox liver, pork and streaky bacon, diced pigeon and garlic. Stir thoroughly over a very low heat. Continue to cook for 1 hour, stirring every 5 minutes and then pour in the brandy, red wine and cream. Season. Transfer the mixture into a pâté dish and place this in a *bain marie*, a roasting dish half filled with water. Cook in pre-heated oven for 1-2 hours. Remove from the oven, allow to set, turn out and decorate. Deep-freezes well.

Pigeon en Croute (Hungry Monk style)

Serves 4

This is a complicated and time-consuming way of cooking pigeon. I include it, firstly because the result is worth the trouble and secondly because cooking buffs may want a recipe into which, so to speak, they can get their teeth.

4 whole pigeons, not just the breasts
4 oz/110 g mushrooms, sliced
2 oz/50 g butter
1 pint mussels (optional)
1 large glass port (approx 4 fl oz/120 ml)
1 lb/450 g puff pastry
1 egg
½ cup milk
salt and pepper, freshly ground

FOR THE SAUCE

1 each onion, carrot, stick of celery
1 each bayleaf, sprig of tarragon, bouquet garni
1 tablespoon each Worcestershire sauce, wine vinegar
1oz/25g tomato purée
2oz/50g butter
2oz/50g flour
freshly-ground salt and black pepper

Remove the breasts from the pigeons, immerse in the port and set aside to marinate for 1½-2 hours.

While the breasts are marinating, prepare the sauce. Chop the carcasses and vegetables, put them in a large pan with the herbs, Worcestershire sauce and wine vinegar, cover with water and bring to the boil. Cover and simmer for 1½ hours. Then strain into a smaller pan and boil rapidly to reduce to 1 pint. In a separate pan melt the butter, add the flour and cook for a few minutes before adding the tomato purée and the pint of pigeon stock. Stir well and set aside.

Lift the pigeon breasts from the marinade and fry with the sliced mushrooms in the butter—3 minutes a side should be ample. Then pour in the port marinade and allow to bubble until the port is reduced to half. Remove the pigeon breasts and set aside. Combine the port marinade and the sauce, pour over the mussels (if included) and blend thoroughly in a food processor. Allow to get quite cold.

Roll out four pastry squares 6"/15 mm x 10"/25 mm, placing two breasts in the centre of each. Spoon the cold sauce over the breasts, damp the edges of the pastry, wrap and seal with egg and milk wash. Allow to stand in the cool for an hour or so before baking in a hot oven (gas mark 7/425°C/220°F) for 20 minutes.

Pigeon Pie (à la Mrs Beeton)

Finally, I thought it might be interesting to see what the great Mrs Beeton had to say about pigeon. I turned not to that mighty tome, *The Book of Household Management*, but to a smaller work, *Mrs Beeton's All About Cookery*, first published in 1897.

The great lady has quite a lot to say about pigeons. She even gives instructions for trussing and carving them. Mrs B. belongs firmly to the boil them or stew them school of thought. Inevitably, Pigeon Pie (Epsom Granstand Recipe) heads the entries, though apparently the race-goers, who dined on what was plainly a traditional dish, liked their pie reinforced with 1½ lb of rump steak and three slices of ham (to two to three pigeons). In terms of pigeon cookery, this does seem to me to verge on cheating. Here, anyway is her Epsom Granstand Pie.

1½ lb rump steak
2 or 3 pigeons
3 slices of ham
2 oz/50 g butter
4 eggs
puff crust
pepper and salt to taste
stock

Cut the steak into 2" squares and line the bottom of the pie dish with it, seasoning well. Clean the pigeons, cut them in half, rub with pepper and salt inside and out, and put into each ½ oz of butter. Lay them on the steak and a piece of ham on each pigeon. Add the yolks of four eggs and half fill the dish with stock. Place a border of puff pastry round the edge of the dish, put on the cover and ornament in any way preferred. Clean three of the birds' feet and place them in a hole made in the crust at the top. This shows what kind of pie it is. Glaze the crust with egg yolk and bake in a well-heated oven for 1½ hours. When liked, a seasoning of pounded mace may be added. Seasonable at any time.

Pigeons Boiled

For those who like their pigeons unadulterated by meat additives, here is something altogether simpler from Mrs Beeton's repertoire.

2 pigeons
2 oz/50 g butter
pepper and salt to taste

Take care that the pigeons are quite fresh and carefully plucked, draw and wash them; split the backs and rub the birds over with butter, season them with pepper and salt, and boil them over a moderate fire for 15 to 20 minutes.

Serve very hot, with either a mushroom sauce or a good gravy. Pigeons may be plainly boiled and served with parsley and butter. They should be trussed like boiled fowls and take from 15 to 20 minutes to boil.

Seasonable from April to September but in greatest perfection from mid-summer to Michaelmas. Cost 1s 8d!

Plucking and Preparing Pigeons

Before you cook your bird, it must be divested from its outer covering. You may be lucky enough always to cook pigeon which other people have prepared for you, or you may already be adept in your own tried and tested ways of preparing pigeon. But I should not like to complete this *Book of the Wood Pigeon* without passing on my own methods, improved and refined over many years, of preparing pigeon for the kitchen.

In the old days, when I used to sell my birds in order to pay some of the cartridge bills for my sons who were then learning to shoot, I oven-readied them. They were delivered neatly plucked, wings, legs and all, which was a fair amount of trouble.

Nowadays, I just take the breasts off the birds. For most recipes this is all you need. I reckon that I can come home with a sack of fifty pigeons and have them packed away, four breasts, the product of two pigeons, to a bag, and in the deep-freeze within an hour, probably less. Moreover, there won't be more than a feather or two to sweep up.

The secret of feather-free plucking is water. If you are granted the privilege, pluck next to the kitchen sink. Only very advanced pluckers will be allowed to do this. If feathers fly, fur is likely to do so also. My wife knows that I am a pleasant, which is to say, tidy plucker and that when I have finished there will not be so much as a single item of down to sully her kitchen floor. It takes years to build up that sort of marital confidence.

If the kitchen is in use, then I pluck in the garage, usually on one of the freezers. My equipment consists of a bowl of water, a long-bladed, sharp kitchen knife and a small pointed ditto. Also, a pair of old garden secateurs or game scissors for cutting through wing roots. Alongside, I have a big kitchen waste bin with an empty liner in it.

Where pigeons are concerned, feathers start to fly from the moment you begin to handle them. When I come in from shooting, I empty the sack (or sacks) straight into the outside game cupboard. This is fitted with slatted shelves on which pigeons can be laid out to cool. This is essential as meat starts to deteriorate, in summer especially, very quickly and the birds will have remained warm through contact in the sack—never a plastic one, please—on the drive home). Having tipped them out, I distribute them on the slatted shelves if I do not intend to pluck them at once and leave them overnight. When I start to pluck, I remove perhaps a dozen pigeons at a time, carrying them to the plucking bench in a box. This again prevents loose feathers from escaping.

Usually, I just 'breast' the birds. I start by dipping my hands in water. Then I pull a few feathers off at the rear end of the breast and dunk them in the bowl of water. With a small pointed knife I nick the skin behind the breast and then simply peel it, with feathers attached, forward over the breast bones, making sure that I ease the skin away from the meat as low as possible, particularly near the wing roots. I do this because when I remove the meat, I don't want any skin still adhering as this requires peeling off later, an unnecessary and fiddly chore.

Now, with the sharp, long-bladed knife I make an incision on one side of the ridge of the breast bone and as close to it as possible. I cut down as near to the bone as I can, at the same time using the flat of the knife blade to ease the meat away from the bone. After that, I just cut the entire breast away at the bottom and repeat the performance on the other side. I have a bowl in which to place the breasts as I remove them.

I then simply drop the remains of the carcase with head, wings and legs attached into the bin liner. Some feathers will inevitably stick to the freed breast meat but don't worry about that. Those can be removed under the tap or in a bowl of clean water before you bag up.

Occasionally, I want to keep the breastbone intact for a dish in which the birds are stuffed with pâté or liver sausage. In that case, I skin as before and cut through the wing roots with the secateurs, ditto the head and neck. I am left with a pigeon 'nugget' inside which any stuffing can be inserted.

When it comes to bagging, I put four breasts per freezer bag, in effect a two-people-meal unit. Young birds, towards the end of harvest mainly, are bagged and labelled separately. They are superbly tender and delicious. Oh yes, the remains! If the waste disposal operatives are due in a day or two, you can tie up the bin liner and hope that they won't notice what is in it. I recall one particularly grisly occasion with the liner had lain uncollected for three hot summer days at the end of which you could actually hear the blowfly maggots rustling inside. If I only have a few corpses and one of the three freezers is 'in ballast', I occasionally, with grudging wifely permission, consign the bin liner to the freezer until 'bin day' comes round again. If you resort to this trick, be sure your wife is fully informed. Mine took out a carrier bag with half a dozen pigeon remains in it under the impression it contained chicken pieces. Black mark!

On that high point I leave you to enjoy all aspects of that great bird, the wood pigeon, not least at your table.

BIBLIOGRAPHY

Arnold, Richard, *Pigeon Shooting*, Faber & Faber, 1961.

Baker, Max, *Sport with Wood Pigeons*, Shooting Times, 1934.

Batley, John, *The Pigeon Shooter*, Swan Hill Press, 1995.

Beeton, Mrs, *All About Cookery*, Ward Lock, 1892.

Coats, Archie, *Pigeon Shooting*, André Deutsch, 1963.

Coats, Prue, *Prue's Country Kitchen*, World Pheasant Association, 1990 and Colt Books Ltd, 1994.

Colquhoun, M.K., *The Wood Pigeon in Britain*, HMSO, 1951.

Cramp, Stanley, *Territorial and other Behaviour of the Wood Pigeon*, Bird Study, 1958.

Ellis, E.A., *The Broads*, Collins New Naturalist, 1965.

Hawker, Coloner Peter, *The Diary of Peter Hawker*, Longmans Green, 1892.

Harradine, John and Nicola Reynolds, *Wood Pigeons, Wood Pigeon Shooting and Agriculture*, Report to BASC Council, 1993.

Humphreys, John, *Shooting Pigeons*, David and Charles, 1988.

Inglis, Ian and A.J. Isaacson, *The Responses of Wood Pigeon to Pigeon Decoys in Various Postures*, MAFF, 1983.

Inglis, Isaacson and R.J.P. Thearle, *Longterm Changes in the Breeding Biology of the Wood Pigeon in Eastern England*, MAFF, 1994.

Lawford, H.F., *The House on Sport*, Gale and Polden, 1898.

Murton R.K., *The Wood Pigeon*, Collins New Naturalist, 1965.

Murton, N.J. Westwood and A.J. Isaacson, *A Study of Wood Pigeon Shooting, The Exploitation of a Natural Animal Population*, MAFF, 1974.

Selby, J.P., *The Naturalist's Library*, 1835.

St John, Charles, *Wild Sport and Natural History of the Highlands*, John Murray, 1892.

Verdet, Pierre, *La Palombe et Ses Chasses*, Edition Deucalion et J. et D. Editions, 1991.

Vesey-Fitgerald, Brian, *British Game*, Collins New Naturalist, 1946.

Walsingham, Lord, *Field and Covert*, Badminton Library, · Longmans Green, 1889.

White, Gilbert, *The Natural History of Selborne*, J.M. Dent, 1976.

Willock, Colin, *The New ABC of Shooting*, André Deutsch, 1994.

INDEX